Frank Richard Stockton

The Christmas Wreck and Other Stories

Frank Richard Stockton

The Christmas Wreck and Other Stories

ISBN/EAN: 9783744705318

Printed in Europe, USA, Canada, Australia, Japan

Cover: Foto ©Thomas Meinert / pixelio.de

More available books at **www.hansebooks.com**

THE
CHRISTMAS WRECK

AND OTHER STORIES

BY

FRANK R. STOCKTON

NEW YORK
CHARLES SCRIBNER'S SONS
1887

COPYRIGHT, 1886, BY
CHARLES SCRIBNER'S SONS.

RAND, AVERY, & CO.,
ELECTROTYPERS AND PRINTERS,
BOSTON.

CONTENTS.

	PAGE
THE CHRISTMAS WRECK	1
A STORY OF ASSISTED FATE. (In two parts) . .	23
AN UNHISTORIC PAGE	66
A TALE OF NEGATIVE GRAVITY	79
THE CLOVERFIELDS CARRIAGE	111
THE REMARKABLE WRECK OF THE "THOMAS HYKE,"	133
MY BULL-CALF	162
THE DISCOURAGER OF HESITANCY.	186
A BORROWED MONTH. (East and West) . . .	196

THE CHRISTMAS WRECK.

"WELL, sir," said old Silas, as he gave a preliminary puff to the pipe he had just lighted, and so satisfied himself that the draught was all right, "the wind's a comin', an' so's Christmas. But it's no use bein' in a hurry fur either of 'em, fur sometimes they come afore you want 'em, anyway."

Silas was sitting in the stern of a small sailing-boat which he owned, and in which he sometimes took the Sandport visitors out for a sail; and at other times applied to its more legitimate, but less profitable use, that of fishing. That afternoon he had taken young Mr. Nugent for a brief excursion on that portion of the Atlantic Ocean which sends its breakers up on the beach of Sandport. But he had found it difficult, nay, impossible just now, to bring him back, for the wind had gradually died away until there was not a breath of it left. Mr. Nugent, to whom nautical experiences were as new as the very nautical suit of blue flannel which he wore, rather liked the calm; it was such a relief to the monotony of rolling waves. He took out a cigar and lighted it, and then he remarked:

"I can easily imagine how a wind might come before you sailors might want it, but I don't see how Christmas could come too soon."

"It come wunst on me when things couldn't a looked more onready fur it," said Silas.

"How was that?" asked Mr. Nugent, settling himself a little more comfortably on the hard thwart. "If it's a story, let's have it. This is a good time to spin a yarn."

"Very well," said old Silas. "I'll spin her."

The bare-legged boy, whose duty it was to stay forward and mind the jib, came aft as soon as he smelt a story, and took a nautical position which was duly studied by Mr. Nugent, on a bag of ballast in the bottom of the boat.

"It's nigh on to fifteen year ago," said Silas, "that I was on the barque, 'Mary Auguster,' bound for Sydney, New South Wales, with a cargo of canned goods. We was somewhere about longitood a hundred an' seventy, latitood nothin', an' it was the twenty-second o' December, when we was ketched by a reg'lar typhoon which blew straight along, end on, fur a day an' a half. It blew away the storm sails; it blew away every yard, spar, shroud, an' every strand o' riggin', an' snapped the masts off, close to the deck; it blew away all the boats; it blew away the cook's caboose, an' every thing else on deck; it blew off the hatches, an' sent 'em spinnin' in the air, about a mile to leeward; an' afore it got through, it washed away the cap'n an' all the crew 'cept me an' two others. These was Tom Simmons, the second mate, an' Andy Boyle, a chap from the Andirondack Mountins, who'd never been to sea afore. As he was a landsman he ought, by rights, to a been swep' off by the wind an' water, consid'rin' that the cap'n an' sixteen good seamen had gone a'ready. But he had hands eleven inches long, an' that give him a grip which no typhoon could git the better of. Andy had let out that his father was a miller up there in York State, an' a story had got round among the crew that his gran'father an' great gran'father was millers too; an' the way the fam'ly got such big hands come from their habit of scoopin' up a extry quart or two of meal or flour for themselves when they was levelin' off their customers' measures. He was a good-natered feller, though, an' never got riled when I'd tell him to clap his flour-scoops onter a halyard.

"We was all soaked, an' washed, an' beat, an' battered. We held on some way or other till the wind blowed itself out, an' then we got on our legs an' began to look about us to see how things stood. The sea had washed into the open hatches till the vessel was more'n half full of water, an' that had sunk her so deep that she must 'a looked like a canal boat loaded with gravel. We hadn't had a thing to eat or drink durin' that whole blow, an' we was pretty ravenous. We found a keg of water which was all right, and a box of biscuit, which was what you might call soft tack, for they was soaked through and through with sea-water. We eat a lot of them so, fur we couldn't wait, an' the rest we spread on the deck to dry, fur the sun was now shinin' hot enough to bake bread. We couldn't go below much, fur there was a pretty good swell on the sea, and things was floatin' about so's to make it dangerous. But we fished out a piece of canvas, which we rigged up agin the stump of the mainmast so that we could have somethin' that we could sit down an' grumble under. What struck us all the hardest was that the barque was loaded with a whole cargo of jolly things to eat, which was just as good as ever they was, fur the water couldn't git through the tin cans in which they was all put up; an' here we was with nothin' to live on but them salted biscuit. There was no way of gittin' at any of the ship's stores, or any of the fancy prog, fur everythin' was stowed away tight under six or seven feet of water, an' pretty nigh all the room that was left between decks was filled up with extry spars, lumber, boxes, an' other floatin' stuff. All was shiftin', an' bumpin', an' bangin' every time the vessel rolled.

"As I said afore, Tom was second mate, an' I was bosen. Says I to Tom, 'the thing we've got to do is to put up some kind of a spar with a rag on it for a distress flag, so that we'll lose no time bein' took off.' 'There's no use a slavin' at anythin' like that,' says Tom, 'fur we've been blowed off the track of traders, an' the more we work the hungrier we'll git, an' the sooner will them biscuit be gone.'

"Now when I heerd Tom say this I sot still, and began to consider. Being second mate, Tom was, by rights, in command of this craft; but it was easy enough to see that if he commanded there'd never be nothin' for Andy an' me to do. All the grit he had in him he'd used up in holdin' on durin' that typhoon. What he wanted to do now was to make himself comfortable till the time come for him to go to Davy Jones's Locker; an' thinkin', most likely, that Davy couldn't make it any hotter fur him than it was on that deck, still in latitood nothin' at all, fur we'd been blowed along the line pretty nigh due West. So I calls to Andy, who was busy turnin' over the biscuits on the deck. ' Andy,' says I, when he had got under the canvas, ' we's goin' to have a 'lection fur skipper. Tom here is about played out. He's one candydate, an' I'm another. Now, who do you vote fur? An', mind yer eye, youngster, that you don't make no mistake.' ' I vote fur you,' says Andy. ' Carried unanermous!' says I. ' An' I want you to take notice that I'm cap'n of what's left of the "Mary Auguster," an' you two has got to keep your minds on that, an' obey orders.' If Davy Jones was to do all that Tom be Simmons said when he heard this, the old chap would kept busier than he ever was yit. But I let him growl his growl out, knowin' he'd come round all right, fur there wasn't no help fur it, consid'rin' Andy an' me was two to his one. Pretty soon we all went to work, an' got up a spar from below which we rigged to the stump of the foremast, with Andy's shirt atop of it.

"Them sea-soaked, sun-dried biscuit was pretty mean prog, as you might think, but we eat so many of 'em that afternoon an' 'cordingly drank so much water that I was obliged to put us all on short rations the next day. ' This is the day before Christmas,' says Andy Boyle, ' an' to-night will be Christmas Eve, an' it's pretty tough fur us to be sittin' here with not even so much hard tack as we want, an' all the time thinkin' that the hold of this ship is packed full of the gayest kind of good things to eat.' 'Shut up about Christmas!' says Tom Simmons. 'Them two youngsters of mine, up in Bangor, is havin' their toes and noses pretty nigh froze, I 'spect, but they'll hang up their stockin's all the same to-night, never thinkin' that their dad's bein' cooked alive on a empty stomach.' 'Of course they wouldn't hang 'em up,' says I, 'if they knowed what a fix you was in, but they don't know it, an' what's the use of grumblin' at 'em for bein' a little jolly.' 'Well,' says Andy, 'they couldn't be more jollier than I'd be if I could git at some of them fancy fixin's down in the hold. I worked well on to a week at 'Frisco puttin' in them boxes, an' the names of the things was on the outside of most of 'em, an' I tell you what it is, mates, it made my mouth water, even then, to read 'em, an' I wasn't hungry nuther, havin' plenty to eat three times a day. There was roast beef, an' roast mutton, an' duck, an' chicken, an' soup, an peas, an' beans, an' termaters, an' plum-puddin', an' mince-pie——' 'Shut up with your mince-pie!' sung out Tom Simmons. 'Isn't it enough to have to gnaw on these salt chips, without hearin' about mince-pie?' 'An' more'n that,' says Andy, 'there was canned peaches, an' pears, an' plums, an' cherries.'

"Now these things did sound so cool an' good to me on that broilin' deck, that I couldn't stand it, an' I leans over to Andy, an' I says: "Now look a here, if you don't shut up talkin' about them things what's stowed below, an' what we can't git at, nohow, overboard you go!' 'That would make you short-handed,' says Andy, with a grin. 'Which is more'n you could say,' says I, 'if you'd chuck Tom an' me over'—alludin' to his eleven-inch grip. Andy didn't say no more then, but after a while he comes to me as I was lookin' round to see if anything was in sight, an' says he, 'I s'pose you ain't got nuthin' to say agin my divin' into the hold just aft of the foremast, where there seems to be a bit of pretty clear water, an' see if I can't git up something?' 'You kin do it, if you like,' says I, 'but it's at your own risk. You can't take out no insurance at this office.' 'All right then,' says Andy, 'an' if I git stove in by floatin' boxes, you an' Tom'll have to eat the rest of them salt crackers.' 'Now, boy,' says I—an' he wasn't much more, bein' only nineteen year old—'you'd better keep out o' that hold. You'll just git yourself smashed. An' as to movin' any of them there heavy boxes, which must be swelled up as tight as if they was part of the ship, you might as well try to pull out one of the "Mary Auguster's" ribs.' 'I'll try it,' says Andy, 'fur to-morrer is Christmas, an' if I kin help it I ain't goin' to be floatin' atop of a Christmas dinner without eatin' any on it.' I let him go, fur he was a good swimmer and diver, an' I did hope he might root out somethin' or other, fur Christmas is about the worst day in the year fur men to be starvin' on, and that's what we was a comin' to.

"Well, fur about two hours Andy swum, an' dove, an' come up blubberin', an' dodged all sorts of floatin' an' pitchin' stuff, fur the swell was still on; but he couldn't even be so much as sartain that he'd found the canned vittles. To dive down through hatchways, an' among broken bulkheads, to hunt fur any partiklar kind o' boxes under seven feet of sea-water, ain't no easy job; an' though Andy says he got hold of the end of a box that felt to him like the big 'uns he'd noticed as havin' the meat pies in, he couldn't move it no more'n if it had been the stump of the foremast. If we could have pumped the water out of the hold we could have got at any part of the cargo we wanted, but as it was, we couldn't even reach the ship's stores, which, of course, must have been mostly spiled anyway; whereas the canned vittles was just as good as new. The pumps was all smashed, or stopped up, for we tried 'em, but if they hadn't a been we three couldn't never have pumped out that ship on three biscuit a day, and only about two days' rations at that.

"So Andy he come up, so fagged out that it was as much as he could do to get his clothes on, though they wasn't much, an' then he stretched himself out under the canvas an' went to sleep, an' it wasn't long afore he was talkin' about roast turkey an' cranberry sass, an' punkin pie, an' sech stuff, most of which we knowed was under our feet that present minute. Tom Simmons he just b'iled over, an' sung out: 'Roll him out in the sun and let him cook! I can't stand no more of this!' But I wasn't goin' to have Andy treated no sech way as that, fur if it hadn't been fur Tom Simmons' wife an' young uns, Andy'd been worth two of him to anybody who was considerin' savin' life. But I give the boy a good punch in the ribs to stop his dreamin', fur I was as hungry as Tom was, and couldn't stand no nonsense about Christmas dinners.

"It was a little arter noon when Andy woke up, an' he went outside to stretch himself. In about a minute he give a yell that made Tom and me jump. 'A sail!' he hollered, 'a sail!' An' you may bet your life, young man, that 'twasn't more'n half a second before us two had scuffled out from under that canvas, an' was standin' by Andy. 'There she is!' he shouted, 'not a mile to win'ard.' I give one look, an' then I sings out: 'Tain't a sail! It's a flag of distress! Can't you see, you land-lubber, that that's the stars and stripes upside down?' 'Why, so it is,' said Andy, with a couple of reefs in the joyfulness of his voice. An' Tom, he began to growl as if somebody had cheated him out of half a year's wages.

"The flag that we saw was on the hull of a steamer that had been driftin' down on us while we was sittin' under our canvas. It was plain to see she'd been caught in the typhoon too, fur there wasn't a mast or a smoke stack on her; but her hull was high enough out of the water to catch what wind there was, while we was so low-sunk that we didn't make no way at all. There was people aboard, and they saw us, an' waved their hats an' arms, an' Andy an' me waved ours, but all we could do was to wait till they drifted nearer, fur we hadn't no boats to go to 'em if we'd a wanted to.

"'I'd like to know what good that old hulk is to us,' said Tom Simmons. 'She can't take us off.' It did look to me somethin' like the blind leadin' the blind; but Andy he sings out: 'We'd be better off aboard of her, fur she aint' water-logged, an', more'n that, I don't s'pose her stores are all soaked up in salt water.' There was some sense in that, and when the steamer had got to within half a mile of us, we was glad to see a boat put out from her with three men in it. It was a queer boat, very low an' flat, an' not like any ship's boat I ever see. But the two fellers at the oars pulled stiddy, an' pretty soon the boat was 'longside of us, an' the three men on our deck. One of 'em was the first mate of the other wreck, an' when he found out what was the matter with us, he spun his yarn, which was a longer one than ours. His vessel was the 'Water Crescent,' nine hundred tons, from 'Frisco to Melbourne, and they had sailed about six weeks afore we did. They was about two weeks out when some of their machinery broke down, an' when they got it patched up it broke agin, worse than afore, so that they couldn't do nothin' with it. They kep' along under sail for about a month, makin' mighty poor headway till the typhoon struck 'em, an' that cleaned their decks off about as slick as it did ours, but their hatches wasn't blowed off, an' they didn't ship no water wuth mentionin', an' the crew havin' kep' below, none on 'em was lost. But now they was clean out of provisions and water, havin' been short when the break-down happened, fur they had sold all the stores they could spare to a French brig in distress that they overhauled when about a week out. When they sighted us they felt pretty sure they'd git some provisions out of us. But when I told the mate what a fix we was in his jaw dropped till his face was as long as one of Andy's hands. Howsomdever he said he'd send the boat back fur as many men as it could bring over, and see if they couldn't get up some of our stores. Even if they was soaked with salt water, they'd be better than nothin'. Part of the cargo of the 'Water Crescent' was tools an' things fur some railway contractors out in Australier, an' the mate told the men to bring over some of them irons that might be used to fish out the stores. All their ship's boats had been blowed away, an' the one they had was a kind of shore boat for fresh water, that had been shipped as part of the cargo, an' stowed below. It couldn't stand no kind of a sea, but there wasn't nothin' but a swell on; an' when it come back it had the cap'n in it, an' five men, besides a lot of chains an' tools.

"Them fellers an' us worked pretty nigh the rest of the day, an' we got out a couple of bar'ls of water, which was all right, havin' been tight bunged; an' a lot of sea biscuit, all soaked an' sloppy, but we only got a half bar'l of meat, though three or four of the men stripped an' dove fur more'n an hour. We cut up some of the meat, an' eat it raw, an' the cap'n sent some over to the other wreck, which had drifted past us to leeward, an' would have gone clean away from us if the cap'n hadn't had a line got out an' made us fast to it while we was a workin' at the stores.

"That night the cap'n took us three, as well as the provisions we'd got out, on board his hull, where the 'commodations was consid'able better than they was on the half-sunk 'Mary Auguster.' An' afore we turned in he took me aft, an' had a talk with me as commandin' off'cer of my vessel. 'That wreck o' yourn,' says he, 'has got a vallyble cargo in it, which isn't spiled by bein' under water. Now, if you could get that cargo into port it would put a lot of money in your pocket, fur the owners couldn't git out of payin' you fur takin' charge of it, an' havin' it brung in. Now I'll tell you what I'll do. I'll lie by you, an' I've got carpenters aboard that'll put your pumps in order, an' I'll set my men to work to pump out your vessel. An' then, when she's afloat all right, I'll go to work agin at my vessel, which I didn't s'pose there was any use o' doin'; but whilst I was huntin' round amongst our cargo to-day I found that some of the machinery we carried might be worked up so's to take the place of what is broke in our engin'. We've got a forge aboard an' I believe we can make these pieces of machinery fit, an' git goin' agin. Then I'll tow you into Sydney, an' we'll divide the salvage money. I won't git nothin' for savin' my vessel, coz that's my bizness; but you wasn't cap'n o' yourn, an' took charge of her a purpose to save her, which is another thing.'

"I wasn't at all sure that I didn't take charge of the 'Mary Auguster' to save myself an' not the vessel, but I didn't mention that, an' asked the cap'n how he expected to live all this time. 'Oh, we kin git at your stores easy enough,' says he, 'when the water's pumped out.' 'They'll be mostly spiled,' says I. 'That don't matter,' says he, 'men'll eat anythin', when they can't git nothin' else.' An' with that he left me to think it over.

"I must say, young man, an' you kin b'lieve me if you know anythin' about sech things, that the idee of a pile of money was mighty temptin' to a feller like me, who had a girl at home ready to marry him, and who would like nothin' better'n to have a little house of his own, an' a little vessel of his own, an' give up the other side of the world altogether. But while I was goin' over all this in my mind, an' wonderin' if the cap'n ever could git us into port, along comes Andy Boyle, and sits down beside me. 'It drives me pretty nigh crazy,' says he, 'to think that to-morrer's Christmas, an' we've got to feed on that sloppy stuff we fished out of our stores, an' not much of it nuther, while there's all that roast turkey, an' plum-puddin', an' mince-pie, a floatin' out there just before our eyes, an' we can't have none of it.' 'You hadn't oughter think so much about eatin', Andy,' says I, 'but if I was talkin' about them things I wouldn't leave out canned peaches. By George! Of a hot Christmas like this is goin' to be, I'd be the jolliest Jack on the ocean if I could git at that canned fruit.' 'Well, there's a way,' says Andy, 'that we might git some of 'em. A part of the cargo of this ship is stuff for blastin' rocks; catridges, 'lectric bat'ries, an' that sort of thing; an' there's a man aboard who's goin' out to take charge of 'em. I've been talkin' to this bat'ry man, an' I've made up my mind it'll be easy enough to lower a little catridge down among our cargo, an' blow out a part of it.' 'What ud be the good of it,' says I, 'blowed into chips?' 'It might smash some,' he said, 'but others would be only loosened, an' they'd float up to the top, where we could get 'em, 'specially them as was packed with pies, which must be pretty light.' 'Git out, Andy,' says I, 'with all that stuff!' An' he got out.

"But the idees he'd put into my head didn't git out, an' as I laid on my back on the deck, lookin' up at the stars, they sometimes seemed to put themselves into the shape of little houses, with a little woman cookin' at the kitchin fire, an' a little schooner layin' at anchor just off shore; an' then agin they'd hump themselves up till they looked like a lot of new tin cans with their tops off, an' all kinds of good things to eat inside, 'specially canned peaches — the big white kind — soft an' cool, each one split in half, with a holler in the middle filled with juice. By George, sir, the very thought of a tin can like that made me beat my heels agin the deck. I'd been mighty hungry, an' had eat a lot of salt pork, wet an' raw, an' now the very idee of it, even cooked, turned my stomach. I looked up to the stars agin, an' the little house an' the little schooner was clean gone, an' the whole sky was filled with nothin' but bright new tin cans.

"In the mornin', Andy, he come to me agin. 'Have you made up your mind,' says he, 'about gittin' some of them good things for Christmas dinner?' 'Confound you!' says I, 'you talk as if all we had to do was to go an' git 'em.' 'An' that's what I b'lieve we kin do,' says he, 'with the help of that bat'ry man.' 'Yes,' says I, 'an' blow a lot of the cargo into flinders, an' damage the "Mary Auguster" so's she couldn't never be took into port.' An' then

I told him what the cap'n had said to me, an' what I was goin' to do with the money. 'A little catridge,' says Andy, 'would do all we want, an' wouldn't hurt the vessel nuther. Besides that, I don't b'lieve what this cap'n says about tinkerin' up his engin'. Tain't likely he'll ever git her runnin' agin, nor pump out the "Mary Auguster" nuther. If I was you I'd a durned sight ruther have a Christmas dinner in hand than a house an' wife in the bush.' 'I ain't thinkin' o' marryin' a girl in Australier,' says I. An' Andy he grinned, an' said I wouldn't marry nobody if I had to live on spiled vittles till I got her.

"A little after that I went to the cap'n, an' I told him about Andy's idea, but he was down on it. 'It's your vessel, an' not mine,' says he, 'an' if you want to try to git a dinner out of her I'll not stand in your way. But it's my 'pinion you'll just damage the ship, an' do nothin'.' Howsomdever I talked to the bat'ry man about it, an' he thought it could be done, an' not hurt the ship nuther. The men was all in favor of it, for none of 'em had forgot it was Christmas day. But Tom Simmons, he was agin it strong, for he was thinkin' he'd git some of the money if we got the 'Mary Auguster' into port. He was a selfish-minded man, was Tom, but it was his nater, an' I s'pose he couldn't help it.

"Well, it wasn't long afore I began to feel pretty empty, an' mean, an' if I'd a wanted any of the prog we got out the day afore, I couldn't have found much, for the men had eat it up nearly all in the night. An' so, I just made up my mind without any more foolin', an' me, and Andy Boyle, an' the bat'ry man, with some catridges an' a coil of wire, got into the little shore boat, and pulled over to the 'Mary Auguster.' There we lowered a small catridge down the main hatchway, an' let it rest down among the cargo. Then we rowed back to the steamer, uncoilin' the wire as we went. The bat'ry man clumb up on deck, an' fixed his wire to a 'lectric machine, which he'd got all ready afore we started. Andy and me didn't git out of the boat; we had too much sense for that, with all them hungry fellers waitin' to jump in her; but we just pushed a little off, an' sot waitin', with our mouths a waterin', for him to touch her off. He seemed to be a long time about it, but at last he did it, an' that instant there was a bang on board the 'Mary Auguster' that made my heart jump. Andy an' me pulled fur her like mad, the others a hollerin' arter us, an' we was on deck in no time. The deck was all covered with the water that had been throwed up; but I tell you, sir, that we poked an' fished about, an' Andy stripped an' went down, an' swum all round, an' we couldn't find one floatin' box of canned goods. There was a lot of splinters, but where they come from we didn't know. By this time my dander was up, an' I just pitched around savage. That little catridge wasn't no good, an' I didn't intend to stand any more foolin'. We just rowed back to the other wreck, an' I called to the bat'ry man to come down, an' bring some bigger catridges with him, fur if we was goin' to do anythin' we might as well do it right. So he got down with a package of bigger ones, an' jumped into the boat. The cap'n he called out to us to be keerful, an' Tom Simmons leaned over the rail, an' swored, but I didn't pay no' tention to nuther of 'em, an' we pulled away.

"When I got aboard the 'Mary Auguster' I says to the bat'ry man: 'We don't want no nonsense this time, an' I want you to put in enough catridges to heave up somethin' that'll do fur a Christmas dinner. I don't know how the cargo is stored, but you kin put one big catridge 'midship, another for'ard, an' another aft, an' one or nuther of 'em oughter fetch up somethin'.' Well, we got the three catridges into place. They was a good deal bigger than the one we first used, an' we j'ined 'em all to one wire, an' then we rowed back, carryin' the long wire with us. When we reached the steamer, me an' Andy was a goin' to stay in the boat as we did afore, but the cap'n sung out that he wouldn't allow the bat'ry to be touched off till we come aboard. 'Ther's got to be fair play,' says he. 'It's your vittles, but it's my side that's doin' the work. After we've blasted her this time you two can go in the boat, an' see what there is to get hold of, but two of my men must go along.' So me an' Andy had to go on deck, an' two big fellers was detailed to go with us in the little boat when the time come; an' then the bat'ry man, he teched her off.

"Well, sir, the pop that followed that tech was somethin' to remember. It shuck the water, it shuck the air, an' it shuck the hull we was on. A reg'lar cloud of smoke, an' flyin' bits of things rose up out of the 'Mary Auguster.' An' when that smoke cleared away, an' the water was all bilin' with the splash of various sized hunks that come rainin' down from the sky, what was left of the 'Mary Auguster' was sprinkled over the sea like a wooden carpet for water birds to walk on.

"Some of the men sung out one thing, an' some another, an' I could hear Tom Simmons swear, but Andy an' me said never a word, but scuttled down into the boat, follered close by the two men who was to go with us. Then we rowed like devils for the lot of stuff that was bobbin' about on the water, out where the 'Mary Auguster' had been. In we went, among the floatin' spars and ship's timbers, I keepin' the things off with an oar, the two men rowin', an' Andy in the bow.

"Suddenly Andy give a yell, an' then he reached himself for'ard with sech a bounce that I thought he'd go overboard. But up he come in a minnit, his two 'leven-inch hands gripped round a box. He sot down in the bottom of the boat with the box on his lap, an' his eyes screwed on some letters that was stamped on one end. 'Pidjin pies!' he sings out. 'Tain't turkeys, nor 'tain't cranberries. But, by the Lord Harry, it's Christmas pies all the same!' After that Andy didn't do no more work, but sot holdin' that box as if it had been his fust baby. But we kep' pushin' on to see what else there was. It's my 'pinion that the biggest part of that bark's cargo was blowed into mince meat, an' the most of the rest of it was so heavy that it sunk. But it wasn't all busted up, an' it didn't all sink. There was a big piece of wreck with a lot of boxes stove into the timbers, and some of these had in 'em beef ready biled an' packed into cans, an' there was other kinds of meat, an' dif'rent sorts of vegetables, an' one box of turtle soup. I looked at every one of 'em as we took 'em in, an' when we got the little boat pretty well loaded I wanted to still keep on searchin', but the men, they said that shore boat ud sink if we took in any more cargo, an' so we put back, I feelin' glummer'n I oughter felt, fur I had begun to be afeared that canned fruit, such as peaches, was heavy, an' li'ble to sink.

"As soon as we had got our boxes aboard, four fresh men put out in the boat, an' after awhile they come back with another load; an' I was mighty keerful to read the names on all the boxes. Some was meat pies, an' some was salmon, an' some was potted herrins, an' some was lobsters. But nary a thing could I see that ever had growed on a tree.

"Well, sir, there was three loads brought in, altogether, an' the Christmas dinner we had on the for'ard deck of that steamer's hull was about the jolliest one that was ever seen of a hot day aboard of a wreck in the Pacific Ocean. The cap'n kept good order, an' when all was ready the tops was jerked off the boxes, and each man grabbed a can an' opened it with his knife. When he had cleaned it out, he tuk another without doin' much questionin' as to the bill of fare. Whether anybody got pidjin pie 'cept Andy, I can't say, but the way we piled in Delmoniker prog would a made people open their eyes as was eatin' their

Christmas dinners on shore that day. Some of the things would a been better, cooked a little more, or het up, but we was too fearful hungry to wait for that, an' they was tip-top as they was.

"The cap'n went out afterwards, an' towed in a couple of bar'ls of flour that was only part soaked through, an' he got some other plain prog that would do fur futur use; but none of us give our minds to stuff like this arter the glorious Christmas dinner that we'd quarried out of the 'Mary Auguster.' Every man that wasn't on duty went below, and turned in for a snooze. All 'cept me, an' I didn't feel just altogether satisfied. To be sure I'd had an A 1 dinner, an' though a little mixed, I'd never eat a jollier one on any Christmas that I kin look back at. But, fur all that, there was a hanker inside o' me. I hadn't got all I'd laid out to git, when we teched off the 'Mary Auguster.' The day was blazin' hot, an' a lot of the things I'd eat was pretty peppery. 'Now,' thinks I, 'if there had a been just one can o' peaches sech as I see shinin' in the stars last night,' an' just then, as I was walkin' aft, all by myself, I seed lodged on the stump of the mizzenmast, a box with one corner druv down among the splinters. It was half split open, an' I could see the tin cans shinin' through the crack. I give one jump at it, an' wrenched the side off. On the top of the first can I seed was a picture of a big white peach with green leaves. That box had been blowed up so high that if it had come down anywhere 'cept among them splinters it would a smashed itself to flinders, or killed somebody. So fur as I know, it was the only thing that fell nigh us, an' by George, sir, I got it! When I had finished a can of 'em I hunted up Andy, an' then we went aft, an' eat some more. 'Well,' says Andy, as we was a eatin', 'how d'ye feel now about blowin' up your wife, an' your house, an' that little schooner you was goin' to own?'

"'Andy,' says I, 'this is the joyfulest Christmas I've had yit, an' if I was to live till twenty hundred I don't b'lieve I'd have no joyfuler, with things comin' in so pat, so don't you throw no shadders.'

"'Shadders,' says Andy, 'that ain't me. I leave that sort of thing fur Tom Simmons.'

"'Shadders is cool,' says I, 'an' I kin go to sleep under all he throws.'

"Well sir," continued old Silas, putting his hand on the tiller and turning his face seaward, "if Tom Simmons had kept command of that wreck, we all would a laid there an' waited an' waited till some of us was starved, an' the others got nothin' fur it, fur the cap'n never mended his engin', an' it was more'n a week afore we was took off, an' then it was by a sailin' vessel, which left the hull of the 'Water Crescent' behind her, just as she would a had to leave the 'Mary Auguster' if that jolly old Christmas wreck had a been there.

"An' now sir," said Silas, "d'ye see that stretch o' little ripples over yander, lookin' as if it was a lot o' herrin' turnin' over to dry their sides? Do you know what that is? That's the supper wind. That means coffee, an' hot cakes, an' a bit of br'iled fish, an' pertaters, an' p'raps — if the old woman feels in a partiklar good humor — some canned peaches, big white uns, cut in half, with a holler place in the middle filled with cool, sweet juice."

A STORY OF ASSISTED FATE.

I.

IN a general way I am not a superstitious man, but I have a few ideas, or notions, in regard to fatality and kindred subjects of which I have never been able entirely to dispossess my mind; nor can I say that I have ever tried very much to do so, for I hold that a certain amount of irrationalism in the nature of a man is a thing to be desired. By its aid he clambers over the wall which limits the action of his intellect, and if he be but sure that he can get back again no harm may come of it, while he is the better for many pleasant excursions.

My principal superstitious notion, and indeed the only one of importance, is the belief that whatever I earnestly desire and plan for will happen. This idea does not relate to things for which people fight hard, or work long, but to those events for which we sit down and wait. It is truly a pleasant belief, and one worthy to be fostered if there can be found any ground for it. I do not exercise my little superstition very often, but when I do I find things happen as I wish;

and in cases where this has not yet occurred there is plenty of time to wait.

I am not a very old person, being now in my twenty-eighth year, but my two sisters, who live with me, as well as most of my acquaintances, look upon me, I think, as an older man. This is not due to my experience in the world, for I have not gone out a great deal among my fellow-men, but rather to my habits of reading and reflection, which have so matured my intellectual nature that the rest of me, so to speak, has insensibly stepped a little faster to keep pace with it. Grace Anna, indeed, is two years older than I, yet I know she looks up to me as a senior quite as much as does Bertha, who is but twenty-four.

These sisters had often laughingly assured me that the one thing I needed was a wife, and, although I never spoke much on the subject, in the course of time I began to think a good deal about it, and the matter so interested my mind that at last I did a very singular thing. I keep a diary, in which I briefly note daily events, especially those which may, in a degree, be considered as epochs. My book has a page for every day, with the date printed at the top thereof; not a very desirable form, perhaps, for those who would write much on one day and very little the next, but it suits me well enough, for I seldom enter into details. Not many months ago, as I sat alone, one evening, in my library, turning over the leaves of this diary, I looked ahead at the pages intended for the days of the year that were yet to come, and the thought entered my mind that it was a slavish thing to be able to note only what had happened, and not to dare to write one word upon the blank pages of the next month, or the next, or even of to-morrow. As I turned backward and forward these pages devoted to a record of the future the desire came to me to write something upon one of them. It was a foolish fancy, perhaps, but it pleased me. I would like a diary, not only of what had been, but of what was to be. I longed to challenge fate, and I did it. I selected a page, not too far ahead and in a good time of the year,— it was September 14th,— and on it I wrote,—

"This day came into my life she who is to be my wife."

When I had made this strange entry I regarded it with satisfaction. I had fully come to the conclusion that it was due to my position as the owner of a goodly estate that I should marry. I had felt that at some time I must do something in this matter. And now a thing was done, and a time was fixed. It is true that I knew no woman who was at all likely, upon the day I had selected, or upon any other day, to exercise a matrimonial influence upon my life. But that made no difference to me. I had taken my fate into my own hands, and I would now see what would happen.

It was then early in July, and in a little more than two months, the day which I had made a very momentous one to me would arrive. I can not say that I had a positive belief that what I had written would occur on the 14th of September, but I had a very strange notion that, as there was no reason why it should not be so, it would be so. At any rate, who could say it would not be so? This sort of thing was not a belief, but to all intents and purposes it was just as good.

It was somewhat amusing even to myself, and it would probably have been very amusing to any one else acquainted with the circumstances, to observe the influence that this foundationless and utterly irrational expectation had upon me. To the great delight of my sisters, I began to attend to matters in which formerly I had taken little interest. I set two men at work upon the grounds about the house, giving my personal supervision to the removal of the patches of grass in the driveway, which led under the oaks to the door. Here and there I had a panel of fence put it better order, and a dead apple-tree, which for some time had stood on the brow of a hill in view of the house, was cut down and taken away.

"If any of our friends think of visiting us," said Bertha, "they ought to come now, while every thing is looking so trim and nice."

"Would you like that?" asked Grace Anna, looking at me.

"Yes," I replied. "That is, they might begin to come now."

At this both my sisters laughed.

"Begin to come!" cried Bertha. "How hospitable you are growing!"

The summer went on, and I kept good faith with my little superstition. If either of us should desert the other, it should not be I who would do it. It pleased me to look forward to the event which I had called up out of the future, and to wait for it — if perchance it should come.

One morning my sister Bertha entered my library, with a letter in her hand and a very pleasant expression on her face. "What do you think?" she said. "We are going to have a visit! — just as the paint is dry on the back porch, so that we can have tea there in the afternoon."

"A visit!" I exclaimed, regarding her with much interest.

"Yes," continued Bertha. "Kitty Watridge is coming to stay with us. I have written and written to her, and now she is coming."

"Who is she?" I asked.

Bertha laughed. "You haven't forgotten the Watridges, have you?"

No, I had not forgotten them; at least, the only one of them I ever knew. Old Mr. Watridge had been a friend of my late father, a cheerful and rather ruddy man, although much given to books. He had been my friend, too, in the days when he used to come to us; and I remember well that it was he who started me on a journey along the third shelf from the top, on the east wall of the library, through "The World Displayed," in many volumes, by Smart, Goldsmith, and Johnson; and thence to some "New Observations on Italy," in French, by two Swedish gentlemen, in 1758; and so on through many other works of the kind, where I found the countries shown forth on their quaint pages so different from those of the same name described in modern books of travel that it was to me a virtual enlargement of the world. It had been a long time since I had seen the old gentleman, and I felt sorry for it.

"Is Mr. Watridge coming?" I asked.

"Of course not," said Bertha. "That would be your affair. And besides, he never leaves home now. It is only Kitty, his youngest daughter, my friend."

I had an indistinct recollection that Mr. Watridge had some children, and that they were daughters, but that was all I remembered about them. "She is grown?" I asked.

"I should think so," answered Bertha, with a laugh. "She is at least twenty."

If my sister could have known the intense interest which suddenly sprung up within me she would have been astounded. A grown-up, marriageable young lady was coming to my house, in September! My next question was asked hurriedly: "When will she be here?"

"She is coming next Wednesday, the 16th," answered Bertha, referring to her letter.

"The 16th!" I said to myself. "That is two days after my date."

"What kind of a lady is she?" I asked Bertha.

"She is lovely, — just as lovely as she can be."

I now began to feel a little disappointed. If she were lovely, as my sister said, and twenty, with good Watridge blood, why did she not come a little sooner? It was truly an odd thing to do, but I could not forbear expressing what I thought. "I wish," I said, somewhat abstractedly, "that she were coming on Monday instead of Wednesday."

Bertha laughed heartily. "I was really afraid," she said, "that you might think there were enough girls already in the house. But here you are wanting Kitty to come before she is ready. Grace Anna!" she cried to my elder sister, who was passing the open door, "he isn't put out a bit, and he is in such a hurry to see Kitty that he thinks she should come on Monday."

It was impossible to chide my sisters for laughing at me, and I could not help smiling myself. "It is not that I am in a hurry to see her," I observed, "for I do not know the young lady at all; but I consider Monday a more suitable day than Wednesday for her arrival."

"It is odd," replied Bertha, "that you should prefer one day to another."

"Is there any reason why it does not suit you to have her come on Wednesday?" asked Grace Anna. "Her visit might be deferred a day or two."

Of course I could give no reason, and I did not wish the visit deferred.

"It's just because he's so dreadfully systematic!" cried Bertha. "He thinks every thing ought to begin at the beginning of the week, and that even a visit should make a fair start on Monday, and not break in unmethodically."

My elder sister was always very considerate of my welfare and my wishes, and had it been practicable I believe that she would have endeavored in this instance to make our hospitality conform to what appeared to be my love of system and order. But she explained to me that, apart from the awkwardness of asking the young lady to change the day which she had herself fixed, without being able to give any good reason therefor, it would be extremely inconvenient for them to have their visitor before Wednesday, as an earlier arrival would materially interfere with certain household arrangements.

I said no more, but I was disappointed; and this feeling grew upon me, for the reason that during the rest of the day and the evening my sisters talked a great deal about their young friend, and I found that, unless they were indeed most prejudiced judges, — which in the case of Grace Anna, at least, I could never believe, — this young person who was coming to us must be possessed of most admirable personal qualities. She was pretty; she had excellent moral sentiments, a well-cultured intellect, and a lovable disposition. These, with the good blood, — which, in my opinion, was a most important requisite, — made up a woman in every way fitted to enter my life in a matrimonial capacity. If, without any personal bias, I had been selecting a wife for a friend, I could not have expected to do better than this. That such a young person should come within the range of my cognizance on the wrong day would be, to say the least, a most annoying occurrence. Why did I not select the 16th, or she the 14th? A fate that was two days slow might as well be no fate at all. My meeting with the girl would have no meaning. I must admit that the more I thought about this girl the more I wished it should have a meaning.

During the night, or perhaps very early in the morning, a most felicitous idea came into my mind. I would assist my fate. My idea was this: On Monday I would drive to Mr. Watridge's house. It was a pleasant day's journey. I would spend Tuesday with him, and, returning on Wednesday, I could bring Miss Kitty with me. Thus all the necessary conditions would be fulfilled. She would come into my life on the 14th, and I would have opportunities of knowing her which probably would not occur to me at home. Everything would happen as it should; only, instead of the lady coming to me, I should go to her.

As I expected, my project, when I announced it at the breakfast table, was the occasion of much mirth, especially on the part of Bertha. "I never saw any thing like it!" she cried. "You want to see Kitty even more than I do. I should never have thought of such a thing as going for her two days in advance."

"As it would have been impossible for you to do so," said I, "I can easily conceive that you would not have allowed the idea to enter your mind."

Grace Anna, however, looked upon my plan with much favor, and entered into its details with interest, dwelling particularly on the pleasure Mr. Watridge would derive from my visit.

I looked forward with great pleasure to the little journey I was about to make. The distance from Eastover, my residence, to Mr. Watridge's house was some twenty-five miles, — a very suitable day's drive in fine weather. The road led through a pleasant country, with several opportunities for pretty views; and about half-way was a neat tavern, standing behind an immense cherry-tree, where a stop could be made for rest and for a midday meal. I had a comfortable, easy-cushioned buggy, well provided with protective appurtenances in case of rain or too much sunshine; and my sisters and myself were of the opinion that, under ordinary circumstances, no one would hesitate between this vehicle and the crowded stage-coach, which was the only means of communication between our part of the country and that in which the Watridge estate lay.

I made an early start on Monday morning, with my good horse, Dom Pedro; named by my sister Bertha, but whether for the Emperor of Brazil, or for a social game of cards which we generally played when we had two or three visitors, and therefore there were too many of us for whist, I do not know. I arrived at my destination towards the close of the afternoon, and old Mr. Watridge was delighted to see me. We spent a pleasant hour in his library, waiting for the return of his two daughters, who were out for a walk. It must be admitted that it was with considerable emotional perturbation that I beheld the entrance into that room of Miss Kitty Watridge. She came in alone; her sister, who was much older, being detained by some household duties, connected, probably, with my unexpected arrival. This, with the action of Mr. Watridge in presently excusing himself for a time, gave me an opportunity, more immediate than I had expected, for an uninterrupted study of this young lady, who had become to me so important a person.

I will not describe Kitty, her appearance, nor her conversation, but will merely remark that before we were joined by her father and sister I would have been quite willing, so far as I was concerned, to show her the entry in my diary.

It may be that a man heavily clad with the armor of reserve and restraint sinks more quickly and deeper than one not so encumbered, when he finds himself suddenly in a current of that sentiment which now possessed me. Be that as it may, my determination was arrived at before I slept that night: Kitty Watridge had entered into my life on the 14th of September, and I was willing to accept her as my wife.

As the son of an old comrade on the part of the father, and as the brother of two dear friends on the part of the daughters, I was treated with hearty cordiality by his family, and the next day was a most pleasing and even delightful one to me, until the evening came. Then a cloud, and a very heavy one, arose upon my emotional horizon. I had stated how I purposed to make the little journey of Miss Kitty to our house more comfortable and expeditious than it would otherwise be, and Mr. Watridge had expressed himself very much pleased with the plan; while Kitty had declared that it would be charming, especially when compared with travel by stage-coach, of which the principal features, in her idea of it, appeared to be mothers, little children, and lunch baskets. But, after dinner, Miss Maria, the elder daughter, remarked very quietly, but very positively, that she did not think it would do — that is the phrase she used — for me to drive her sister to Eastover. She gave no reasons, and I asked none, but it was quite evident that her decision was one not to be altered.

"It would be far better," she said, "not to change our original plan, and for Kitty, as well as her trunk, to go by the stage. Mrs. Karcroft is going the whole of the way, and Kitty will be well taken care of."

Miss Maria was the head of the house; she had acted for many years as the maternal director of her sister; and I saw very soon that what the other two members of the family might think upon the subject would matter very little. The father, indeed, made at first some very vigorous dissent, urging that it would be a shame to make me take that long drive home alone, when I had expected company; and although Kitty said nothing, I am sure she looked quite disappointed. But neither words nor looks availed any thing. Miss Maria was placid, but very firm, and under her deft management of the conversation the subject was soon dismissed as settled.

"I am very sorry," observed the old gentleman to me, when the ladies had bidden us good-night, "that Kitty can not take advantage of your invitation, which was a very kind one, and to which I see not the slightest objection. My daughter Maria has very peculiar ideas sometimes, but as she acts as a sort of mother here we don't like to interfere with her."

"I would not have you do so for the world," answered I.

"You are very good, very good!" exclaimed Mr. Watridge; "and I must say I think it's a confounded shame that you and Kitty can not take that pleasant drive together. Suppose you go with her in the stage, and let me send a man to Eastover with your horse and vehicle."

"I thank you very kindly, sir," I replied, "but it will be better for me to return the way I came; and your daughter will have a companion, I understand."

"Nobody but old Mrs. Karcroft, and she counts for nothing as company. You had better think of it."

I would not consent, however, to make any change in my arrangements; and, shortly after, I retired.

I went to bed that night a very angry man. When I prepared a plan or scheme with which no reasonable fault could be found, I was not accustomed to have it thwarted, or indeed even objected to. I was displeased with Mr. Watridge because he allowed himself to be so easily influenced, and I was even dissatisfied with Kitty's want of spirit, though of course she could not have been expected to exhibit an eagerness to accompany me. But with that horrible old maid, Miss Maria, I was truly indignant. There frequently arises in the mind an image which forcibly connects itself with the good or bad qualities of a person under our contemplation, and thus Miss Maria appeared to me in the character of a moral pepper-box. Virtue is like sugar or cream,—good in itself, and of advantage to that with which it is suitably mingled; but Miss Maria's propriety was the hottest and most violent sort of pepper, extremely disagreeable in itself, and never needed except in the case of weak moral digestion. Her objections were an insult to me. I went to sleep thinking of a little pepper cruet which I would like to have made of silver for my table, to take the place of the owl or other conventional pattern, which should be exactly like Miss Maria, — hard and unimpressionable without, hollow within, and the top of its head perforated with little holes. At breakfast I endeavored to be coldly polite, but it must have been easy for the family to perceive that I was very much offended. I requested that my horse and buggy should be made ready as soon as possible. While I was waiting for it on the porch, where Mr. Watridge had just left me, Miss Kitty came out to me. This was the first time I had been alone with her since the preceding afternoon, when we had had a most charming walk through the orchard and over the hills to a high point, where we had stayed until we saw the sun go down.

"It seems a real pity," she observed very prettily, and in a tone which touched me, "that you should be driving off now by yourself, while in about an hour I shall start from the same place."

"Miss Kitty," said I, "would you like to go with me?"

She hesitated for a moment, looked down, and then looked up, and said, "So far as I am concerned, I think — I mean I know — that I should like very much to go with you. But you see" — and then she hesitated again.

"Say no more, I pray you!" I exclaimed. I would not place her in the unpleasant position of defending, or even explaining, the unwarrantable interference of a relative. "If you really wish to accompany me," I continued, warmly shaking her hand, for my buggy was now approaching, "I am entirely satisfied, and nothing more need be said. It is, in a measure, the same as if you were going with me. Good-by."

A moment before I was depressed and morose. Now I was exuberantly joyful. The change was sudden, but there was reason for it. Kitty wished to go with me, and had come to tell me so!

Mr. Watridge and his elder daughter now appeared in the doorway, and as I took leave of the latter I am sure she noticed a change in my manner. I said no more to her than was absolutely necessary, but the sudden cheerfulness which had taken possession of me could not be repressed even in her presence.

The old gentleman accompanied me to the carriage-block. "I don't want to bore you about it," he said, "but I really am sorry you are going away alone."

I felt quite sure, from several things Mr. Watridge had said and done during my visit, that he would be well pleased to see his younger daughter and myself thrown very much into the company of each other, and to have us remain so, indeed, for the rest of our lives. And there was no reason why he should not desire it. In every way the conditions of such a union would be most favorable.

"Thank you very much," I returned; "but the pleasure of having your daughter at my house will make me forget this little disappointment."

He looked at me with glistening eyes. Had I boldly

asked him, "Will you be my father-in-law?" no more favorable answer could have come from his lips than I now saw upon his countenance.

"Good fortune be with you!" were his last words as I drove away.

I do not suppose anything of the kind could be more delightful than my drive that morning. Miss Kitty had said that she would like to be my companion, and I determined to have her so in imagination, if not in fact. The pleasures of fancy are sometimes more satisfactory than those of reality, for we have them entirely under our control. I chose now to imagine that Miss Kitty was seated by my side, and I sat well to the right, that I might give her plenty of room. In imagination I conversed with her, and she answered me as I would have her. Our remarks were carefully graduated to the duration of our acquaintance and the seemly progress of our intimacy. I wished to discover the intellectual status of the fair young creature who had come into my life on the 14th of September. I spoke to her of books, and found that her reading had been varied and judicious. She had read Farrar's "Life of Christ," but did not altogether like it; and while she had much enjoyed Froude's "Cæsar," she could have wished to believe the author as just as he endeavored to make his hero appear. With modern romance she had dealt but lightly, rather preferring works of history and travel, even when pervaded with the flavor of the eighteenth century. But we did not always speak of abstract subjects; we were both susceptible to the influences of nature, and my companion enjoyed as much as I did the bright sunshine tempered by a cooling breeze, the clear sky with fair white clouds floating along the horizon, and the occasional views of the blue and distant mountains, their tops suffused with warm autumnal mists. After a time I asked her if I might call her Kitty, and glancing downward, and then up, with the same look she had given me on the porch, she said I might. This was very pleasant, and was not, in my opinion, an undue familiarity, which feature I was very careful to eliminate from our companionship. One act, however, of what might be termed superfriendly kindness, I intended to propose, and the contemplation of its probable acceptance afforded me much pleasure. After our quiet luncheon in the shaded little dining-room of the Cherry-Tree Inn, and when she had rested as long as she chose, we would begin our afternoon journey, and the road, before very long, would lead us through a great pine wood. Here, rolling over the hard, smooth way, and breathing the gentle odor of the pines, she would naturally feel a little somnolent, and I intended to say to her that if she liked she might rest her head upon my shoulder, and doze. If I should hear the sound of approaching wheels I would gently arouse her; but as an interruption of this kind was not likely to occur, I thought with much satisfaction of the pleasure I should have in the afternoon, when this fancy would be appropriate. To look upon the little head gently resting on that shoulder, which, when our acquaintance had more fully developed, I would offer her as a permanent possession, would be to me a preconnubial satisfaction of a very high order.

When about a mile from the Cherry-Tree Inn, and with my mind filled with these agreeable fancies, an accident happened to me. One of the irons which connected the shafts to the front axle broke, and the conditions of my progress became abruptly changed. The wheel at that end of the axle to which a shaft was yet attached went suddenly forward, and the other flew back and grated against the side of the buggy, while both wheels, instead of rolling in the general course of the vehicle, were dragged in a sidewise direction. The disconnected shaft fell upon the legs of Dom Pedro, who, startled by the unusual sensation, forsook his steady trot, and broke into a run. Thus, with the front wheels scraping the road, the horse attached but by a single shaft, I was hurried along at an alarming pace. Pull as I might, I could not check the progress of Dom Pedro; and if this state of affairs had continued for more than the few moments which it really lasted, the front wheels would have been shattered, and I do not know what sad results might have ensued. But the other shaft broke loose, the reins were rudely torn from my hands, and the horse, now free from attachment to the vehicle, went clattering along the road, the shafts bobbing at his heels; while the buggy, following the guidance of the twisted front axle, ran into a shallow ditch at the side of the road, and abruptly stopped.

Unhurt, I sprang out, and my first thought was one of joy that the Kitty who had been by my side was an imaginary one. Had the real Kitty been there, what might not have happened to her! A dozen possible accidents crowded themselves on my mind, and I have no doubt my countenance expressed my feelings.

There was nothing to be done but to take my valise and the whip from the buggy, and walk on to the inn, where I found the landlord in the act of saddling a horse, to come and see what had happened to me. Dom Pedro had arrived with a portion of the shafts attached to him, the rest having been kicked away. The accident occasioned considerable stir at the inn; but as I never cared to discuss my personal affairs any further than is necessary, it was soon arranged that after I had lunched I would borrow a saddle from the landlord, and ride Dom Pedro home, while the broken buggy would be brought to the inn, where I would send for it the next day. This plan did not please me, for I was not fond of equestrianism, and Dom Pedro was rather a hard trotter; but there was nothing better to do. Had I not taken this road, which was much more agreeable although rather longer than the high road, I might have been picked up by the stage which was conveying Miss Kitty to my house.

While I was yet at my meal there arrived at the inn a young man, who shortly afterward entered the room, and informed me that, having heard of my accident, he came to offer me a seat in the buggy in which he was traveling. He was going my way, and would be glad of a companion. This invitation, given as it was by a well-appearing young man of pleasing manners, was, after a little consideration, accepted by me. I would much prefer to ride a dozen miles in a buggy with a stranger than on horseback alone.

The drive of the afternoon was very different from what I had expected it to be, but it was not devoid of some pleasant features. My companion was sociable, and not too communicative; although he annoyed me very much by giving me the entirely uncalled-for information that if I had had short straps from the ends of the shafts to the axle, which no well-ordered buggy should be without, the accident would not have occurred. I passed this by, and our conversation became more general, and to me more acceptable. The young man was going to Harnden, a village not far from my house, where he appeared to have some business, and he assured me that he would not object in the least to go a little out of his way and set me down at my door.

We reached Eastover quite late in the afternoon, and I perceived, from the group on the porch, that Miss Kitty had arrived. All three of the ladies came down to meet me, evidently very much surprised to see me in a strange vehicle. When I alighted, and was hastily explaining to my sisters the cause of this change of conveyance, I was surprised to see Miss Kitty shaking hands with the young man, who was standing by his horse's head. My elder sister, Grace Anna, who had also noticed this meeting, now approached the pair, and was introduced to the gentleman. In a few moments she returned to me, who had been regarding the interview with silent amazement.

"It is Harvey Glade," she said, — "Kitty's cousin. We should invite him to stay here to-night."

I can not conceive of anything which more quickly

than these words would have snuffed out the light which had illumined the vision of my house with Kitty in it; but it was impossible for me to forget that I was a gentleman and the master of Eastover, and, instantly causing my perception of these facts to take precedence of my gathering emotions, I stepped up to Miss Kitty, and, asking to be introduced to her cousin, I begged him to make my house his home during his stay in the neighborhood.

This invitation was accepted, as I supposed it would be when I made it; yet I must own that I did not expect Mr. Glade to remain at my house for a week. Of course his presence prevented the execution of any of my plans regarding the promotion of my intimacy with Kitty; but although the interruption caused me much vexation, I maintained the equanimity due to my position, and hoped each day that the young man would take his leave. Towards the end of his visit I became aware, through the medium of my sisters, to whom I had left in a great degree the entertainment of our guests, that young Glade was actually engaged to be married to Kitty. She had told them so herself. This statement, which chilled to the verge of frigidity my every sensibility, was amplified as follows: The young people had been attached to each other for some time, but the visits of Glade having been discouraged by Miss Kitty's family, they had not seen each other lately, and there had been no positive declaration of amatory sentiment on the part of either. But this protracted sojourn in my house had given the young man all the opportunity he could desire, and the matter was settled so definitely that there was no reason to suppose that the better judgment of her elders would cause the young woman to change her mind.

Here was a fine ending to my endeavors to assist my fate. Instead of so doing, I had assisted the fate of Mr. Harvey Glade, in whose welfare I had no interest whatever. He had not known that Miss Kitty was coming to my house; he had not even been aware, until he met her at Eastover, that I was acquainted with her family. Had it not been for my endeavors to promote my own fortune in the direction of the lady, he would have had no opportunity to make her his own; and they probably would not have seen each other again, unless he had happened to call upon her as the mistress of Eastover. Instead of aiding Miss Kitty to enter my life on the 14th of September, I had ushered her into his life on the 16th of that month.

For a week after the departure of our guests — the young man went first — I found myself in a state of mental depression from which the kindly efforts of my sisters could not arouse me. Not only was I deeply chagrined at what had occurred, but it wounded my self-respect to think that my fate, which had been satisfactorily pursuing the course I had marked out for it, should have been thus suddenly and disastrously turned aside. I felt that I must confess myself conquered. It was an unusual and a difficult thing for me to do this, but there was no help for it. I took out my diary, and turned to the page whereon I had challenged fate. That entry must be erased. I must humble myself, and acknowledge it untrue.

At the moment that I dipped the pen in the inkstand there was a knock at the door, and Grace Anna entered.

"I have just had a letter," she said, "from dear Jane Wiltby, who married your old schoolfellow, Dr. Tom. I thought you would like to hear the news it contains. They have a little girl, and she is to be named for me."

"How old is it?" I asked, with indifferent interest.

"She was born on the 14th of September," said Grace Anna.

I sat erect, and looked at my sister — looked at her without seeing her. Thoughts, like clouds upon the horizon brightened by the rays of dawn, piled themselves up in my mind. Dr. Tom, the companion of my youth, ever my cherished friend! Jane, woman above women! Grace Anna!

I laid down the pen, and, leaving the momentous and prognostic entry just as I had written it, I closed my diary, and placed it in my desk.

He who can not adapt himself to the vagaries of a desired fate, who can not place himself upon the road by which he expects it to come, and who can not wait for it with cheerful confidence is not worthy to be an assistant arbiter of his destiny.

II.

The fact that on the day indicated in my diary a young creature not only came into my life, but into her own, greatly satisfied and encouraged me. I would begin at the beginning. Within the sphere of my immediate cognizance would grow and develop the infant, the child, the girl, the woman, and, finally, the wife. What influence might I not have upon this development? The parents were my friends; the child was my selected bride. The possibilities of advantageous guidance, unseen perhaps, but potent to a degree unattainable by a mere parent or guardian, were, to my thinking, boundless.

I was now more content than I had been in the case of the young lady whom I had supposed had been given me by Fate, but who, it now appeared very fortunately, had been snatched away before my irrevocable mistake had been made. I was very grateful for this: I was grateful to Fate; I was grateful to Mr. Glade, the successful lover; I was even grateful to Kitty for not having allowed herself to be influenced by anything she may have seen in me during our short acquaintance. Of the past of Kitty I knew little, as was well demonstrated by the appearance of Harvey Glade. My present *fiancée* had no past. With her and with me it was all future, which would gently crystallize, minute by minute and day by day, into a present which would be mutually our own.

Of course I said nothing of all this to any one. The knowledge of our destiny was locked up in the desk which held my diary and in my own heart. When the proper time came, she, first, should know. I am an honorable man, and as such felt fully qualified to be the custodian of what was, in fact, her secret as well as mine.

I took an early opportunity to become acquainted with the one who was to be the future partner of my life. It was towards the end of October, I think, that I paid a visit to Dr. Tom Wiltby and his wife Jane, my predestined parents-in-law. Had they known the position they occupied towards me, they would have been a very much surprised couple. The interest I exhibited in their first-born did, as I thought, surprise them a little, but it only increased the warmth of the welcome they gave me, and drew me closer to their hearts. The emotions which possessed me when, in the preceding summer, I had stood awaiting the moment when Kitty Watridge should enter the room and first present herself to my sight were nothing to those which quickened the action of my heart as a nurse brought into the Wiltby parlor a carefully disposed bundle of drapery, in the midst of which reposed my future wife.

I approached, and looked at her. Her face was displayed to view, but her form was undistinguishable. For an instant our eyes met; but, so far as I could judge, no spark of reciprocal sympathy seemed to shine from hers. In fact, they rolled about in an irrelevant manner which betokened a preoccupation so intense that even the advent of a husband could have no effect upon it. But whatever the child had on its mind — or stomach — gave a volcanic mobility to its countenance, which caused me much to wonder. The eyes then closed, and appeared to be writhing and swelling beneath their lids; the mouth was alternately convoluted and unrolled towards nose, cheeks, and chin; while the rest of the face, which had been of an Indian reddish hue, now darkened, and from the puffy jaws to the top of the bald head seemed moved by a spasm, but whether of premonition or despair I could not tell.

I withdrew my gaze. It might be well that I should wait for a time before allowing my eyes to feed upon this countenance.

I went away a little disappointed. The chaoticness of initiatory existence had never before been so forcibly impressed on my mind.

During the following winter and spring I built up an ideal, or rather a series of ideals. They were little children, they were girls, they were women. At about nineteen years of age the individual existence of each ended, and became merged into the oneness of my matrimonial life. Sometimes my ideal was a blonde, sometimes a brunette. From the cursory glance I had had of the one to whom all these fancies referred, I could not judge whether she would be dark or fair. She had no hair, and all that I could remember of her eyes was that they had no soul light. Her father was dark, her mother fair: she might be either.

Of all the legendary heroines of love, none ever so impressed me as that Francesca whose strong love not only braved every prejudice and barrier of earth, but, according to eye-witnesses of the fact, floated with her indefinitely through hell. In verse and picture, and upon the stage, I knew Francesca well, — better, perhaps, than any other woman. But to such an one I would not be merely a Paolo, but the elder brother also. I would have no proxy, no secret love, no unfaithfulness. There should be all the impetuosity, all the spirit of self-immolation, without any necessity for it. She who was to be mine had become in my thoughts a Francesca, and she grew before my mind to ripened loveliness. Her eyes sparkled with rapture when, as through the gates of old Ravenna, the fair Ghibelline first saw the brave rider that she thought to wed, so this one would see through the gates of womanly consciousness, not a mere envoy, but both Malatesta brothers in one, — lover and husband, — me. With such an imaginary one I read legends of old loves; with such an one I sat in shaded bowers, her young face upturned to mine, and the red light from the wings touching with color the passionate picture. But no jester watched with sneering gibes, no husband fought afar on battle-field; Paolo and Lanciotto in one looked into the uplifted eyes.

It was in the early summer that my two sisters and myself were invited to the Wiltby mansion for a visit, which our kindly hosts hoped would be somewhat protracted. Among other things that were to be done the baby was to be baptized, and Grace Anna, for whom she was named, was to act as godmother. I was very glad to make this visit. Quite a long time had now elapsed since my first interview with Francesca, as I always intended to call her, notwithstanding the name that might be bestowed upon her by the church; and she must have now begun to foreshadow, in a measure, that which she was to be.

When I saw her I found that there was not quite so much foreshadowing as I had expected; but, in spite of that, she was a little creature whom, without doing violence to any æsthetic instinct, I could take to my heart. She was a pudgy infant, with blue eyes, a blankety head, and a mouth that was generally ready to break into a smile if you tickled the corners of it. Instead of the long and flowing draperies in which I first beheld her, she now wore short dresses, and that she possessed remarkably fat legs and blue woolen socks was a fact which Francesca never failed to endeavor to impress upon my observation. I excited a great deal of surprise, with some admiration on the part of the mother and occasional jocular remarks from Bertha, my younger sister, by showing, at the very beginning of our visit, a strong preference for the society of the baby. I asked to be allowed to take her into my arms, and walk with her into the garden; and although this privilege was at first denied me, unless some lady should accompany me, I being considered quite inexperienced in the care of an infant, I at last gained my point, and frequently had the pleasure of a *tête-à-tête* stroll with Francesca. With my future bride in my arms, slowly walking in the shaded avenues of the garden, I gave my imagination full play. I enlarged her eyes, and gave them a steadiness of upturn which they did not now possess; the white fuzz upon her head grew into rich masses of gold-brown hair; the nose was lengthened and refined; her lips were less protruded, and made more continuously dry; while a good deal of fatty deposit was removed from the cheeks and the second chin. As I walked thus tenderly gazing down upon her, and often removing her little fist from her mouth, I pictured in her lineaments the budding womanhood for which I waited. I would talk softly to her, and although she seldom answered but in a gurgling monotone I saw in our intercourse the dawning of a unity to be.

After we had been a few days at the Wiltby house Miss Kitty Watridge came there, also on a visit. Her engagement to Mr. Glade had not produced much effect upon her personal appearance, although I thought her something quieter, and with a little sedateness which I had not observed in her before. Her advent at this time was not to my liking. As an object of my regard, she had, in becoming engaged to another, ceased to exist; she had passed out of my sphere of consideration, and the fact that she had once acted a prominent part within it made it appear to me that propriety demanded that she should not only go out of it, but stay out of it. Her influence upon my intercourse with Francesca was, from the first, objectionable. My sisters had always been accustomed to regard my wishes with a gratifying respect, and Mrs Wiltby seemed anxious to imitate them in this laudable action. But Miss Watridge had apparently no such ideas, and she showed this most objectionably by imagining that she had as much right to the baby as I had. Of course she could not understand how matters stood, — nobody but myself could understand that; but she had not the native delicacy of perception of my sisters and Jane Wiltby. She could not know in how many ways she interfered with my desires and purposes. My morning walks were, in a manner, broken up; for sometimes the new-comer actually insisted upon carrying the baby herself, in which case I retired, and sought some other promenade. But after a few days I found that the indulgence of any resentment of this sort not only made me the object of remark, but promised to entirely break up my plans in regard to Francesca. I wished to create in my mind while here such an image of her, matured and perfected according to my own ideas, that I could live and commune with her during the absences, more or less protracted, which must intervene before the day when I should take her wholly to myself. As I could not expect to stay here very much longer, I must not lose what opportunities I had, and so concluded to resume my walks with Francesca, even if Miss Watridge should sometimes intrude herself upon us.

I must admit, however, that this she did not do, considering the matter with strict regard to fact. She generally possessed herself of the baby, and if I wished its company I was obliged to intrude myself upon her. The plan I now adopted was, I think, somewhat ingenious. As is my wont, I endeavored to shape to my advantage this obstacle which I now found in my way. My intercourse with Francesca had not been altogether satisfactory. For one thing, there had been too much unity about it. A certain degree of this was, indeed, desirable, but I was obliged to be, at once, not only husband and lover, but lady also; for Francesca gave me no help in this regard, except, perchance, an occasional look of entreaty, which might as well mean that she would like a bottle of milk as that she yearned for fond communion of the soul. When I addressed her as my developed ideal I imagined her answers, and so continued the gentle conversation; but, although she always spoke as I would wish, there were absent from our converse certain desirable elements which might have been looked for from the presence of a second intellect. Another source of dissatisfaction was that in many of our interviews Francesca acted in a manner which was not only disturbing, but indecorous. Frequently, when I was speaking with her on such subjects as foreign travel, when we two would wander amid the misty purples of Caprian sunsets, or stand together in vast palaces of hoarded art, she would struggle so convulsively, and throw upward with such violence her small blue socks, that, for the time, I wished she was swaddled and bound in the manner of the Della Robbia babies on the front of the Foundling Asylum in Florence.

A plan of relieving myself from the obvious disadvantages of my present method of intercourse with an intellect, a soul, and a person, which to be suitable for my companionship must necessarily be projected into the future, now suggested itself to me. If Miss Watridge persisted in forcing herself upon Francesca, she might at least make herself useful by taking the place of that young person so far as regarded a part in the conversation. Her entity occupied a position in respect to growth and development which was about the same as that to which I was in the habit of projecting Francesca. Her answers to my remarks would be analogous, if not similar, to those which might be expected from the baby when she arrived at maturity. Thus, in a manner, I could talk to Francesca, and receive her answers from the lips of Miss Kitty. This would be as truly love-making by proxy as when the too believing Lanciotto sent from Rimini his younger brother to bear to him Ravenna's pearl. But here was no guile, no dishonesty; the messenger, the vehicle, the interpreter, in this case, knew nothing of the feelings now in action, or to be set in action, of the principals in the affair. She did not know, indeed, that there were two principals. As far as she herself was concerned, she had, and could have, no interest in the matter. She was engaged to be married to Mr. Glade, which, in my eyes, was the same thing as being already married to him; and any thoughts or mental emotions that she might have relating to affectionate interest in one of the opposite sex would of course be centered in Mr. Glade. With Francesca and myself she would have nothing to do but uncon-

sciously to assist in the transmission of sentiment.
Had Paolo been engaged to marry a suitable young
person before he started for Ravenna, it is probable that
the limited partnership which Dante noticed in the
Inferno would never have been formed.

It was by slow degrees, and with a good deal of
caution, that I began my new course of action. Taking the child in my arms, I invited Miss Watridge to
accompany us in our walk. Thus, together, we slowly
strolled along the garden avenue, shaded by the fresh
greenness of June foliage, and flecked here and there
by patches of sunlight, which moved upon the gravel
in unison with the gentle breeze. Our conversation,
at first relating to simple and every-day matters, was
soon directed by me into a channel in which I could
perceive whether or not I should succeed in this project
of representative rejoinder. It was not long before I
was pleased to discover that the mind of the young
lady was of as good natural quality and as well cultivated as I had formerly supposed it to be; having then
little upon which to base my judgment, except the
general impression which her personality had made
upon me. That impression having been entirely effaced, I was enabled with clearer vision and sounder
judgment to determine the value of her mental exhibit.
I found that she had read with some discrimination,
and with a tendency to independent thought she united
a becoming respect for the opinions of those who, by
reason of superior years, experience, and sex, might
be supposed to move on a psychological plane somewhat higher than her own. These were dispositions

the development of which I hoped to assist in the young Francesca, and it may be imagined that I was much gratified to find my model so closely resembling that personality which I wished, in a manner, to create.

Thus, up and down, daily, would we stroll and talk. With the real Francesca on my arm, sometimes sleeping, and sometimes indulging in disturbing muscular exercises, which I gently endeavored to restrain, I addressed myself to my ideal Francesca, an aerial maiden, garbed in simple robes of white touched by a soft suggestion of Italian glow, and ever with tender eyes upturned to mine; while from her proxy, walking by my side, came to me the thoughts and sentiments of her fresh young heart.

It was quite natural that I should be more interested in a conversation of this kind than in one in which I was obliged to supply the remarks on either side. To be sure, in the latter case, there was a unison of thought between myself and the ideal Francesca that was very satisfactory, but which lacked the piquancy given by unexpectedness of reply and the interest consequent upon gentle argument.

It so happened that the morning occupations of Mrs. Wiltby and my sisters were those in which Miss Watridge did not care to join, and thus she was commonly left free to make one of the company of four which took its morning walks upon the garden avenue. I imagine that she supposed it was generally thought that she was taking care of the baby and affording it advantages of out-door air, in the performance of which pleasing duty my presence was so unnecessary that the probability of it was not even considered. Thus it was that upon every fair day—and all those days were fair—our morning strolls were prolonged for an hour or more, generally terminated only by the culminating resolve of Francesca to attract to herself so much attention that a return to the house was necessary. It may be supposed that it would have been better to have eliminated the element of the actual being from the female side of our little company. But that side, several as it was in its component personages, represented to me the one Francesca; and had I not held and felt the presence of the actual living creature, who was to be and to say all that my mind saw and my ear heard, I could not have spoken as I wished to speak to the ideality who was to be my wife when it became a reality. The conjunction seemed to me a perfect one, and under the circumstances I could wish for nothing better.

As our acquaintance ripened and mellowed in the pleasant summer days, I was enabled to see more clearly into the soul and heart of the Francesca that was to be, looking at them through the transparent mind of Miss Kitty Watridge. According to the pursuance of my plan, I gradually, and as far as possible imperceptibly, changed the nature of our converse. From talking of the material world, and those objects in it which had pleased our vision or excited reflection, we passed to the consideration, very cursory at first, of those sentiments which appear to emanate from ourselves without the aid of extraneous agency. Then, by slow degrees, the extraneous agency was allowed to enter upon the scene, coming in so quietly that at first it was scarcely noticeable. The dependence of man upon man was discussed, not only for material good, but for intellectual support and comfort. Then, following a course not exactly in accordance with that of nature, but which suited my purposes, we spoke of social ties, — of the friendships which spring up here and there from these; of the natural affections of the family; and, finally, the subject arising in consistent sequence, of that congruent intermental action of the intellect of two persons, generally male and female, who frequently, without family ties of any kind and but little previous acquaintanceship, find, each in the other, an adaptiveness of entity which is mutually satisfactory.

The vicarious replies of Francesca were, in almost every instance, all that I could have wished. Sometimes there were symptoms of hesitancy or reluctance in the enunciation of what was, obviously, the suitable reply to some of my remarks in regard to the deeper sentiments; but, on the whole, had the ideal lady of my love spoken to me, her words could not have better aroused my every sentiment of warm regard.

Sometimes I wondered, as thus we walked and talked, what Mr. Glade would think about it if he could see us so much together, and listen to our converse. But this thought I put aside as unworthy of me. It was an insult to myself as an honorable man; it was an uncalled-for aspersion on Miss Watridge, and a stain upon my idealistic intercourse with Francesca. If Mr. Glade was coarse and vulgar enough to interject his personality into this perfectly working system of intellectual action, from which the individuality of Miss Watridge was entirely eliminated, her part in it being merely to represent another, I could not help it. It was this consciousness of rectitude, this probity of purpose, which raised our little drama so far above the level of the old story of the wedded Guelph and Ghibelline.

With my mind satisfied on this subject, I did not hesitate, when the proper time seemed to have arrived, to allow myself to imagine Francesca at the age of nineteen. I could not much longer remain in this place, as we had now overstayed the original limit of our visit; and there was danger, too, that Miss Watridge might be called away. I wished, while the opportunity continued, to develop the imaginary life of Francesca into perfect womanhood, so that I could carry away with me an image of my future wife, which I could set upon the throne of my affection, there to be revered, cherished, and guarded, until the time came when the real Francesca should claim the seat. Of course, under these circumstances, a certain fervor of thought and expression was not only necessary, but excusable, and I did not scruple to allow it to myself. Always with the real Francesca in my arms, in order that even my own superconscientiousness might not take me to task, I delivered my sentiments without drawing the veil of precautionary expression over their amatory significance. It was at this stage of our intercourse that I asked Miss Watridge to allow me to call her Francesca; for it was only by so doing that I could fully identify her voice with that of the visionary creature who was now exciting the stirring impulses of my heart. When she asked me why I wished to call her by this name, I could only tell her that it was for ideal purposes; and without making further inquiries, she consented that I should use it — for the present. As it was only for the present that I thought of so doing, this much of acquiescence was sufficient, and I called her by the name I loved.

The softly-spoken, well-considered replies, the gentle ejaculations, and the demure but earnest attention which my speech elicited well befitted the fairest vision of pure young womanhood that my soul could call before me. But, notwithstanding this, there was something wanting. I longed for the upturned eyes, ever fixed upon my own, of the Francesca of the stage. I longed for the fair white hands clasped and trembling as I spoke. I longed for that intensity of soul-merge in which the loved one breathes and lives only that she may hear the words I speak, and watch the thoughts that fashion in my face. Without all this I could never take away with me the image of the true Francesca. Without this there would be wanting, in the fair conception, that artistic roundness, that completeness of outline and purpose, which would satisfy the exigencies of my nature. I could not consent to carry with me for years an ideal existence, incomplete, imperfected, — a statue devoid of those last touches of the master which make it seem to live.

Therefore I sought, with much earnestness and

fixity of intention; to call up the last element needed to complete that lovely creation which was to be my companion through the years of waiting for the real Francesca. It was a great comfort and support to me to reflect that I could do this with such safety, with such unusual advantages. I addressed myself to no being in existence. Even the little creature on my arm, who had fallen into a habit of dozing when not noticed, and to whom belonged, in fact, my every gift and legacy of love, was not of age to come into her fortune, nor could her infantile mind be injured by its contemplation. And as for Miss Watridge, she, as I continually repeated to myself, was acting simply as the representative of another, and her real self was not concerned in the little drama, in which she did not even take a part; merely assuming, as in a rehearsal, a character which another actor, not able then to be present, would play in the actual performance.

It was the loveliest morning of all the summer that I made my supreme effort. At the very bottom of the garden was a little arbor of honeysuckles. No crimson stage-light shone in upon it, but the sunbeams pushed their way here and there through the screen of leaves, and brightened the interior with points of light. It was a secluded spot, to which I had never yet led my companions, for the period had not before arrived for such sequesterment. But now we sat down here upon a little bench: I at one end, the young Francesca on my knee, and Miss Watridge at my left. In the place where this lady sat also sat the ideal Francesca, occupying the same space, and endowed, for the time, with the same form and features. It was to this being that I now addressed my fervid words; low-burning, it is true, but alive with all the heat and glow that precedes blaze. I told a tale; not reading from pages of mediæval script the legend of the love of Launcelot and Queen Guinevere, as does Paolo in the play, but relating a story which was a true one, for it was my own. I spoke as I expected to speak some day to the little creature on my knee. Taking with my disengaged hand that of the lady by my side, I said that which raised a lovely countenance to mine, that showed me the beauty of her upturned eyes; and as I looked and spoke I felt that the very pulses of her soul were throbbing in accord with mine. Here was enacting in very truth the scene I had viewed upon the stage, and which so often since had risen before my fancy. Possessed by the spirit of this scene, carried onward by that same tide of passional emotion the gradual rise of which it had portrayed, I gave myself up to its influences, and acted it out unto its very culmination. I stooped, and, in the words of the Arthurian legend, "I kissed her full upon the mouth."

Swift as the sudden fall of summer rain, I felt the wild abandonment of clinging arms about my neck, of tears upon my face that were not mine, of words of love that I spoke not; and it came to me like a flash that she who clung to me, and around whom my arm was passed, was Kitty Watridge, and not a visionary Ghibelline.

In the midst of my varying emotions I clasped closer to me the real Francesca, who thereupon gave vent to her feelings by parting wide her toothless gums, and filling the summer air with a long yell. At this rude interruption, the arms fell from my neck, and the face was quickly withdrawn from mine.

Now came hurrying steps upon the gravel walk, and my sister Bertha ran in upon us. "What on earth are you doing to that baby?" she cried. She snatched the child from me, and then stood astonished, gazing first at me and then at Kitty, who had started to her feet, with sparkling tears still in her eyes and a sunset glow upon her face. Without a word, the wicked Bertha laughed a little laugh, and, folding the child within her arms, she ran away.

I sat speechless for a moment, and then I turned to Kitty; but she, too, had gone, having fled in another direction. I was left alone: gone was the real Francesca; gone was the fair ideal; gone was Kitty. I stood bewildered, and, in a manner, dazed. I felt as if I had fallen from the fourteenth century into the nineteenth, and that the shock had hurt me. I felt, too, a sense of culpability, as if I had been somewhere where I had no right to be; as if I had been a trespasser, a poacher, an intruder upon the times or on the rights of others. The fact that I was a strictly honorable man, scorning perfidy in its every form, made my feelings the more poignant. A little reflection helped me to understand it all. I had carried out my plan so carefully, with such regard to its gradual development, that by degrees Miss Watridge had grown into the ideal Francesca, and had to all intents and purposes gone back with me into the Middle Ages, in order to better portray my perfected ideal. The baby sitting on my right knee, while a future stage of her life was being personated by the lady at my side, might belong to any age; there was nothing incongruous in her presence on the scene. It was the entrance of my sister Bertha that broke the spell, that shattered the whole fabric I had so elaborately built. She was of the present, of to-day, of the exact second, in which she helped anything to happen. An impersonation of the Now, her coming banished every idea of the Past or Future.

Like an actor in a play, on whom his every-day clothes and the broad light of day have suddenly fallen, I walked slowly to the house. Meeting my older sister, Grace Anna, near the door, I took her aside, and said to her, "When is Mr. Glade expected here?"

"What for?" she asked, with eyes dilated.

"To marry Kitty Watridge," said I.

"What do you mean?" exclaimed my sister. "That match was broken off last winter."

It may well be supposed that, remembering what Bertha had seen, and doubtless imagined; that remembering what Kitty had done and said; and recalling, too, how I felt when she did it and said it, I resolved, instead of waiting eighteen long years for another, to accept as the Francesca of my dreams, and as the veritable wife of my actual existence, this dear girl, who was able to represent at this very present the every attribute and quality of my ideal woman.

In the autumn we were married. Thus my Fate, disclaiming my efforts to assist it, no matter in what direction, rose dominant, and, attending to my affairs in its own way, gave me Kitty at last.

But I shall always feel sorry for the baby.

AN UNHISTORIC PAGE.

AN elderly negro man, Uncle Enoch by name, short of stature and with hair and beard beginning to grizzle, but with arms and body yet stout and strong, stood back of his little log house, not far from a Virginia public road, endeavoring to pull his ax out of a knotty black-gum log. Often and often, when his stock of firewood had diminished to this one log, had Uncle Enoch tried to split it, and now he was trying again. While thus engaged, there came to him his son Dick. This was a youth rather taller and lighter in color than his father, of an active and good-natured disposition, and hitherto supposed to be devoid of disturbing ambitions.

"Look a-heah, daddy," said he, "won't yuh lemme go to Washin'ton nex' week?"

Uncle Enoch stopped tugging at his ax, and turned round to look at Dick. "What fur?" said he.

"I'se gwine to be a page in Congress."

"What's dat?" asked his father, his bright eyes opening very wide. "What yuh want to do dat fur?"

"A page is one of dem chaps as runs round and

AN UNHISTORIC PAGE. 67

waits on de Congressmen, when dey're doing dere work in Washin'ton. Dere's lots of 'em, and some of 'em is culle'd. Dey hab to be mighty peart and cut around, and fetch de Congressmen eberyting dey wants. And dey don't have to work for no fifty cents a day, nudder. Dey gits sebenteen hunderd dollars a year."

"What's dat?" exclaimed Uncle Enoch. "Yuh means de whole kit and boodle uv 'em gits dat."

"No, I don't," said Dick. "Ebery one gits it for hisse'f."

"Yuh shu'h ob dat?"

"Yes, sah," replied Dick. "I heerd it all from a man down at de cross-roads, when I took ole Billy to be shod dis ebenin'. He wus tellin' a lot o' folks all about it at de stoah. An' won't yuh lemme go nex' week?"

The old man put his hand on his ax-handle and stood reflectively.

Uncle Enoch had been born a slave, and had been an honest and industrious servant, whose only failing was that he was inclined to think himself better at all times, and to dress himself better on Sundays, than his companions; and now that he was as free as anybody, he was still honest and industrious, and still went to church with the highest white hat, the biggest shirt collar, and the longest coat of anybody in the congregation. As he grew older, his opinion of himself did not decrease, and he was very fond of exhorting his fellow-members in church, and of giving them advice in private whenever he saw cause for it, and this very often in the shape of some old fable, which generally became strangely twisted as it passed through the old man's mental organism.

"Look a-heah, Dick," said he, "I'se gwine ter tell yuh a story. It's one uv ole Mahsr George's stories, and I've heerd him tell it often to the chillun. Dere was a mouse what lived in de city, I dunno 'zactly whar, but jus' as like as not it was Washin'ton, an' he went to see a friend uv hisn who had a plantation. De plantation mouse he were glad to see de udder one, an' put him in de cump'ny chahmber, an' gib him de bes' he had; but de fine gemman he didn't 'pear to be satisfy wid nuffin but light bread an' cohn pone for breakfus', an' chicken an' ham for dinner, and he says, says he, —

"'Yuh don' git canvis-back ducks down heah, I reckin?'

"'No, sah!' ses de plantation mouse.

"'Nur tar'pins, stewed in Madary wine?'

"'No, sah!'

"'Nur eysters, fresh from de bay ebery mawnin'; nur ice-cream, all de colors ob de rainbow; an' little candy-balls, what go off pop when you pull 'em; an' a whole bottle ob champain to each pusson?'

"'No, *sah!*' ses de plantation mouse, a-fannin' ob hisse'f wid he han'kercher.

"'Well, now, jus' yuh look a-heah,' ses de udder one, gwine out on de poach to smoke his cigar, ' yuh come to de city an' see me, and when you tase what dem dar tings is like, yuh won't be content fur to stay no more on dis yere no-count farm, so fur from de railroad.'

"So, soon as he sell he 'baccer, de plantation mouse he go to see his city fren'. He glad to see him, an' sot him right down to a pow'ful good dinner, wid all de canvis-back ducks an' de tar'pins an' de eysters an' de champain, an' de udder tings dat he done tell 'bout.

"'If I'd a-knowed you wus a-comin',' ses de city mouse, 'I'd had a reg'lar cump'ny dinner; but yuh'll have to go 'long and jus' take pot-luck wid us dis time.'

"'Den you didn't git my letter?' ses de plantation mouse.

"'No, sah. Reckin yuhr man done forgot to put it in de pos'-office.'

"So dey sot an' eat till dey mos' like to bus', an' de plantation mouse he wonner what he would a-had if he fren' had done got he letter.

"Jus' as dey was litin' dere cigars, and puttin' dey heels up on two cheers, de dinin'-room door open, an' in walk de sheriff ob de county.

"'Look a-heah, kurnel,' ses he, 'have yuh got de money ready fur all de ducks an' de eysters an' de wine you've had fur yuhse'f; an' de slab meat an' de cohn from de West fur yuhr han's? Yuh know I said I wouldn't give yuh no longer nur ter-day.' De city mouse he turn pale, an' he tuk de plantation mouse into one corner, an' ses he, —

"'Look a-heah, kin yuh len' me two or free tousand dollars till to-morrer mawnin', when de bank opens?'

Den de udder mouse he pull a dreffrul poor mouf, an' he ses, —

"'I'se pow'ful sorry, but it rained so much in de

low groun's las' year dat my cohn wus all spiled; an' dere wasn't no rain on de high groun's, an' de cohn dere wus all wilted; an' de fros' done cotch my baccer craps, an' I didn't have money enuf fur to buy quinine fur de han's.'

"Den de town mouse he ses to de sheriff, ses he, —

"'You call aroun' Monday mawnin', an' I'll pay yuh dat money. I wus a'spectin' my fren' ter-day, and done forgot to k'lect it.'

"'Dat won't do,' ses de sheriff. 'I'se heerd dat story often 'nuf.' An' he rung he auction bell, an' he lebied on eberyting in de house; an' as dey didn't fotch enuf, he sold dat city mouse an' dat plantation mouse fur slaves."

Dick uttered an exclamation of horror at this direful conclusion of the story.

"Now look a-heah, boy," continued Uncle Enoch, "ef yuh tinks yuh is gwine down to Washin'ton to git tar'pins an' oysters an' champain out ob dem Congressmen, yuh won't be tuk an' sold, 'cause dey can't do dat now, but yuh'll find yuhse'f gobbled up some way wuss dan dat plantation mouse wus."

Dick grumbled that he wasn't a mouse, and he wasn't "gwine arter tar'pins, nur oysters, nudder."

"Jus' yuh go 'long an' pick up some chips an' trash fur to make de fire," said his father, "an' don't talk to me no mo'h ob dat foolishness."

Dick walked slowly off to do as he was bid, and for a long time Uncle Enoch remained standing by the twisted black-gum log without striking it a blow.

Uncle Enoch was a skillful and practised ox-driver,

working in that capacity for the farmer on whose land he lived. All the next day he walked meditatively by the side of the slowly-moving Bob and Blinker, hauling wood from the mountain. He did not shout as much as usual to his oxen, but he guided them with all his customary precision around stumps, rocks, and the varied impediments of the rough woodland road.

"Yuh Dick," said he to his son in the evening, "is yuh done gib up all dat foolishness 'bout goin' to Washin'ton?"

"'Taint no foolishness," muttered Dick.

"Why, boy," said his father, "'pears to me yuh is too ole for dat sort o' ting."

"It don't make no kind o' diff'rence how ole a page is," said Dick. "Dat man said so hisse'f. He ses dey got 'em all ages."

"Dat so, shuh?" asked his father.

"Sartin shuh," said Dick.

"And dey gits sebenteen hunderd dollars a year?"

"Yes," said Dick. "An' besides dat, dey can make lots ob money blackin' boots an' holdin' hosses an' runnin' arrants fur de Congressmen, when court's out."

Uncle Enoch looked steadfastly at his son for some moments without speaking. Then he said, "Look a-heah, boy; I'se made up my mind 'bout dis yere business. Ef all dat 'ar money's to be got by pageiu', I agrees to de notion."

"Hi-yi!" shouted Dick, beginning to dance.

"Yuh needn't cut up no sich capers," said his father. "*Yuh* aint gwine. I'se gwine mese'f."

If Dick could have turned pale, he would have done so. He stood speechless.

"Yes, sah," continued Uncle Enoch. "Ef it don't make no difference how ole de pages is, I kin step roun' as lively as any uv 'em, an' kin wait on de Congressmen better'n any boy. I knows what de gemmen wants, an' I knows how to do it. I'se waited on 'em 'fore yuh was bawn, boy, an' yuh neber libed 'mong white folks, nohow. Jus' yuh take dat ox-whip termorrer mawnin', an' tell Mahsr Greg'ry dat I'se done gone to Washin'ton, and dat yuh've come to drive de oxen. Yuh's ole enuf fur dat now, an' it's time yuh was beginnin'."

Downcast as Dick was when he heard that he was not going to be a page in the halls of Congress, his spirits immediately rose when he was told that he was to take Uncle Enoch's place as ox-driver. To crack the long whip, and guide the slow progress of Bob and Blinker, was to him a high delight and honor which impressed him the more forcibly because it was so totally unexpected. The Government position had held forth glittering advantages, which had greatly attracted him, but which his mind did not entirely comprehend. But to drive the oxen was a real thing, a joy and a dignity which he knew all about. Dick was entirely satisfied. As to the page's salary which his memory or his ears had so greatly exaggerated, he did not even think of it.

Uncle Enoch determined not to announce his intention to his neighbors, nor to take counsel of any one. He went into the house, and after electrifying his family with the statement of his intended step into what was to them wealth and high position, he set them all to work to get him ready for an early start the next morning. Washing, ironing, patching and packing went on during a great part of the night; his wife, "Aunt Maria," his three daughters, and even Dick, doing their utmost to fit him out for his great undertaking.

"What I'se gwine to do wid dat sebenteen hunderd dollars," said Uncle Enoch, as he sat on a low chair sewing up a gap in one of his Sunday boots, "is to buy dis track o' land on de hill back heah, an' make a wine-yard uv it. No use foolin' no more wid little tater patches, an' cabbyges, an' tree or foh dozen hills o' cohn; I'll sell de grapes, an' buy all dat sort o' ting. At de wine-cellar in town dey'll take all de grapes yoh kin raise, an' ef I have to buy a hoss an' wagun to haul 'em inter town, yuh won't see dis yere fam'ly walkin' to church no mo'h wid de mud up to dere knees and de hot sun brilin' on ter dere heads."

A little after daylight the next morning Uncle Enoch, wearing his tall white hat with the broad band of crape around it which it had on when it was given to him; with his highest and stiffest shirt-collar; a long black coat reaching nearly to his heels; a pair of blue jean trousers rolled up at the ankles; his enormous Sunday boots well blacked; in one hand a very small cowhide trunk tied up with a rope and carried in the manner of a violin-case; a vast umbrella with a horn handle in the other hand, and the greater part of his recently paid month's wages in his pocket, started off to walk three miles to the railroad-station on his way to become a Congressional page.

Dick assumed the ox-whip, and as there was no one else to take the vacated place, he cracked it in pride and glory over the heads of Bob and Blinker, and, although they ran into more stumps, and got into more deep ruts, than was good for themselves or the cart, the winter wood of Mr. Gregory continued to be hauled.

One week, and two weeks, passed on without news from Uncle Enoch, and then Aunt Maria began to get impatient. "Look a-heah, Dick," she said, "when you comes home ter-night, an' has had yuhr supper, an' has done split up dem ole rails, what's too short fur de fence anyway, fur 'taint no use fur yuh to try no mo'h on dat black-gum log what yuh daddy done went away and luf, an' ef he don't come back soon he won't find no fence at all, I reckin, when he do come, yuh jus' sot down an' write him a letter, an' tell him 'taint no use fur him to be sabin up all dat sebenteen hunderd dollars to buy wine-yards while his chillun's gwine about wid scace no close to dere backs.

"Dere's yuhr sis'r Charlotte what has to go to church wid dem light-blue slippers Miss Sally gib her, an' no stockuns, an' no wunner de people laf at her. An' dere's yuhr daddy makin' all dat money down dere in Washin'ton wid de Congressmen.

"An' she a gal, too, what's done won de prize tree times in de cake-walk. I spec' he's done forgot what I tole him 'bout de weddin'-ring fur me. I done tole him to buy it wid de fus' money he got an' to send it in a letter. I'se neber had none yit, though we wus both married long back befoh de war.

"An' it's no use waitin', nudder, fur little Jim's funeral till he comes back. He kin sen' de money fur de cake and wine jus' as well as not, an' Brudder Anderson is ready, he tole me las' Sund'y, wid de fax an' de tex. Little Jim's been dead now nigh on ter two yeah, an' it's time his funeral was preached.

"I ain't got no 'jections to de wine-yard, spesh'ly ef we hab ter hab a wagun to haul de grapes, but I don't want yuhr daddy to come back heah an' find hissef 'shamed uv his fam'ly arter livin' down dar 'mong all dem quality folks. I'll send Charlotte dis mawnin' to borrer a sheet uv paper, an' a pen an' ink from Miss Sally, an' see ef she won't let her pick up some apples in de orchard while she's dar, an' p'raps she'll give her a bucket uv buttermilk ef she's done churned yistiddy. An' yuh put all dat in de letter, an' sen' it off jus' as soon as yuh kin."

Dick willingly undertook this business, having made up his mind while his mother was talking to him to put in a few words on his own account; and before he began the important epistle each of his sisters had something to say to him in private in regard to suggestions which they wished him to make to the head of the family.

The letter moved more slowly than Bob and Blinker over the roughest road. After three nights' work it was only half-done, for Dick found a pen much more difficult to handle than a whip, and besides being a very stumbling speller, invariably went to sleep over his paper after a quarter of an hour's work. Late in the afternoon of the fourth day after the commencement of this literary enterprise, Dick was standing by the black-gum log, with the axe in his hand, wondering if it would be better to take another rail from the forlorn fence around the little yard — for what difference could it make when there were so many open places already? — or to split up a solitary post, which having nothing attached to it was clearly useless, when he saw upon the high-road a figure approaching him.

It wore a tall white hat with a broad band of rusty crape around it; it had on a high stiff shirt-collar, and a long black coat; in one hand it carried an umbrella with a rough horn handle, and in the other a little hair trunk tied up with a rope; it had a bright and flashing eye, and a determined step.

It did not go on to the house, but, turning from the public road, came through a gap in the fence, and walked straight up to the astonished Dick.

"Look a-heah, yuh Dick," said Uncle Enoch, putting down his little trunk; "who done tole yuh all dat foolishness about gwine to Washin'ton to wait on de Congressmen, an' gittin' sebenteen hunderd dollars a yeah?"

"It wus a man at de cross-roads," said Dick, "wid a red beard. He done brung some hosses ober from de Cou't House. I dunno his name."

"Is he bigger nur yuh is?" asked his father.

"Oh yes," said Dick, "more'n twice as big."

"Well, den, yuh luf him alone," said Uncle Enoch,

with great decision and energy, "yuh luf him alone. I hopes, boy," the old man continued, wiping his face with his great blue and yellow handkerchief, "dat yuh's gwine ter larn a lesson from dis yere bis'ness. It makes me tink ob two no-'count beasts dat wus once loafin' in a little clearin' dat had bin buhned fur a seed-patch. Dey wus stannin' in de sun to warm deyse'fs, bein' too pow'ful lazy to cut some wood and make a fire. One was a gy-raffe, an' de udder was a kangerroo. De gy-raffe he look at de kangerroo, an' he begun to larf.

"'It's mighty cur'us,' ses he, 'to see a pore critter like yuh, wid some legs short and some legs long. Ef I was yuh I'd go to de wood-pile, an' I'd chop dem hine legs off de same lent as de foh ones, so yuh'd go about like common folks, an' not be larfed at.'

"Dese remarks dey make de har riz on de kangerroo's back, he so mad angry.

"'Yuh suh'tinely is a gay boy,' ses he to de gy-raffe, 'to stan' up dere an' preach like dat, wid yer hine legs short as plow-hannels an' yuhr foh legs too long fur butter-bean poles, so dat yuhr back slopes down like de roof of a ice-house. Ef I wus yuh I'd go to de wood-pile, an' I'd chop off dat ar long neck close to de head, I'd be so 'shamed.'

"Now, boy," continued Uncle Enoch, "dere's lots ob stories about one eberlastin' fool, but dat's de only story I knows 'bout two uv 'em. An' now jes' yuh go inter de house, an' tell de folks I'se gwine ter put a new cracker on de ox-whip, an' ef any ob dem ses Washin'ton to me, I'll make 'em dance Jerusalem!"

Dick walked into the house to deliver this message, and as he went, he said to himself, "I reckin de plantation mouse done gin up he wine-yard."

A TALE OF NEGATIVE GRAVITY.

MY wife and I were staying at a small town in northern Italy; and on a certain pleasant afternoon in spring we had taken a walk of six or seven miles to see the sun set behind some low mountains to the west of the town. Most of our walk had been along a hard, smooth highway, and then we turned into a series of narrower roads, sometimes bordered by walls, and sometimes by light fences of reed, or cane. Nearing the mountain, to a low spur of which we intended to ascend, we easily scaled a wall about four feet high, and found ourselves upon pasture land, which led, sometimes by gradual ascents, and sometimes by bits of rough climbing, to the spot we wished to reach. We were afraid we were a little late, and therefore hurried on, running up the grassy hills, and bounding briskly over the rough and rocky places. I carried a knapsack strapped firmly to my shoulders, and under my wife's arm was a large, soft basket of a kind much used by tourists. Her arm was passed through the handles, and around the bottom of the basket, which she pressed closely to her side. This was the way she always carried it. The basket contained two bottles of wine, one sweet for my wife, and another a little acid for myself. Sweet wines give me a headache.

When we reached the grassy bluff, well known thereabouts to lovers of sunset views, I stepped immediately to the edge to gaze upon the scene, but my wife sat down to take a sip of wine, for she was very thirsty; and then, leaving her basket, she came to my side. The scene was indeed one of great beauty. Beneath us stretched a wide valley of many shades of green, with a little river running through it, and red-tiled houses here and there. Beyond rose a range of mountains, pink, pale-green, and purple where their tips caught the reflection of the setting sun, and of a rich gray-green in shadows. Beyond all was the blue Italian sky, illumined by an especially fine sunset.

My wife and I are Americans, and at the time of this story were middle-aged people and very fond of seeing in each other's company whatever there was of interest or beauty around us. We had a son about twenty-two years old, of whom we were also very fond, but he was not with us, being at that time a student in Germany. Although we had good health, we were not very robust people, and, under ordinary circumstances, not much given to long country tramps. I was of medium size, without much muscular development, while my wife was quite stout, and growing stouter.

The reader may, perhaps, be somewhat surprised that a middle-aged couple, not very strong, or very good walkers, the lady loaded with a basket containing two bottles of wine and a metal drinking-cup, and the gentleman carrying a heavy knapsack, filled with all sorts of odds and ends, strapped to his shoulders, should set off on a seven-mile walk, jump over a wall, run up a hill-side, and yet feel in very good trim to enjoy a sunset view. This peculiar state of things I will proceed to explain.

I had been a professional man, but some years before had retired upon a very comfortable income. I had always been very fond of scientific pursuits, and now made these the occupation and pleasure of much of my leisure time. Our home was in a small town; and in a corner of my grounds I built a laboratory, where I carried on my work and my experiments. I had long been anxious to discover the means, not only of producing, but of retaining and controlling, a natural force, really the same as centrifugal force, but which I called negative gravity. This name I adopted because it indicated better than any other the action of the force in question, as I produced it. Positive gravity attracts everything toward the center of the earth. Negative gravity, therefore, would be that power which repels everything from the center of the earth, just as the negative pole of a magnet repels the needle, while the positive pole attracts it. My object was, in fact, to store centrifugal force and to render it constant, controllable, and available for use. The advantages of such a discovery could scarcely be described. In a word, it would lighten the burdens of the world.

I will not touch upon the labors and disappointments of several years. It is enough to say that at last I discovered a method of producing, storing, and controlling negative gravity.

The mechanism of my invention was rather complicated, but the method of operating it was very simple. A strong metallic case, about eight inches long, and half as wide, contained the machinery for producing the force; and this was put into action by means of the pressure of a screw worked from the outside. As soon as this pressure was produced, negative gravity began to be evolved and stored, and the greater the pressure the greater the force. As the screw was moved outward, and the pressure diminished, the force decreased, and when the screw was withdrawn to its fullest extent, the action of negative gravity entirely ceased. Thus this force could be produced or dissipated at will to such degrees as might be desired, and its action, so long as the requisite pressure was maintained, was constant.

When this little apparatus worked to my satisfaction I called my wife into my laboratory and explained to her my invention and its value. She had known that I had been at work with an important object, but I had never told her what it was. I had said that if I succeeded I would tell her all, but if I failed she need not be troubled with the matter at all. Being a very sensible woman, this satisfied her perfectly. Now I explained everything to her, the construction of the machine, and the wonderful uses to which this invention could be applied. I told her that it could diminish, or entirely dissipate, the weight of objects of any kind. A heavily loaded wagon, with two of these instruments fastened to its sides, and each screwed to a proper force, would be so lifted and supported that it would press upon the ground as lightly as an empty cart, and a small horse could draw it with ease. A bale of cotton, with one of these machines attached, could be handled and carried by a boy. A car, with a number of these machines, could be made to rise in the air like a balloon. Everything, in fact, that was heavy could be made light; and as a great part of labor, all over the world, is caused by the attraction of gravitation, so this repellent force, wherever applied, would make weight less and work easier. I told her of many, many ways in which the invention might be used, and would have told her of many more if she had not suddenly burst into tears.

"The world has gained something wonderful," she exclaimed, between her sobs, "but I have lost a husband!"

"What do you mean by that?" I asked, in surprise.

"I haven't minded it so far," she said, "because it gave you something to do, and it pleased you, and it never interfered with our home pleasures and our home life. But now that is all over. You will never be your own master again. It will succeed, I am sure, and you may make a great deal of money, but we don't need money. What we need is the happiness which we have always had until now. Now there will be companies, and patents, and lawsuits, and experiments, and people calling you a humbug, and other people saying they discovered it long ago, and all sorts of persons coming to see you, and you'll be obliged to go to all sorts of places, and you will be an altered man, and we shall never be happy again. Millions of money will not repay us for the happiness we have lost."

These words of my wife struck me with much force. Before I had called her my mind had begun to be filled and perplexed with ideas of what I ought to do now that the great invention was perfected. Until now the matter had not troubled me at all. Sometimes I had gone backward and sometimes forward, but, on the whole, I had always felt encouraged. I had taken great pleasure in the work, but I had never allowed myself to be too much absorbed by it. But now everything was different. I began to feel that it was due to myself and to my fellow-beings, that I should properly put this invention before the world. And how should I set about it? What steps should I take? I must make no mistakes. When the matter should become known hundreds of scientific people might set themselves to work; how could I tell but that they might discover other methods of producing the same effect. I must guard myself against a great many things. I must get patents in all parts of the world. Already, as I have said, my mind began to be troubled and perplexed with these things. A turmoil of this sort did not suit my age or disposition. I could not but agree with my wife that the joys of a quiet and contented life were now about to be broken into.

"My dear," said I, "I believe, with you, that the thing will do us more harm than good. If it were not for depriving the world of the invention I would throw the whole thing to the winds. And yet," I added, regretfully, "I had expected a great deal of personal gratification from the use of this invention."

"Now, listen," said my wife, eagerly, "don't you think it would be best to do this: use the thing as much as you please for your own amusement and satisfaction, but let the world wait. It has waited a long time, and let it wait a little longer. When we are dead let Herbert have the invention. He will then be old enough to judge for himself whether it will be better to take advantage of it for his own profit, or simply to give it to the public for nothing. It would be cheating him if we were to do the latter, but it would also be doing him a great wrong if we were, at his age, to load him with such a heavy responsibility. Besides, if he took it up, you could not help going into it, too."

I took my wife's advice. I wrote a careful and complete account of the invention, and, sealing it up, I gave it to my lawyers to be handed to my son after my death. If he died first, I would make other arrangements. Then I determined to get all the good and fun out of the thing that was possible without telling any one anything about it. Even Herbert, who was away from home, was not to be told of the invention.

The first thing I did was to buy a strong leathern knapsack, and inside of this I fastened my little machine, with a screw so arranged that it could be worked from the outside. Strapping this firmly to my shoulders, my wife gently turned the screw at the back until the upward tendency of the knapsack began to lift and sustain me. When I felt myself so gently supported and upheld that I seemed to weigh about thirty or forty pounds, I would set out for a walk. The knapsack did not raise me from the ground, but it gave me a very buoyant step. It was no labor at all to walk; it was a delight, an ecstasy. With the strength of a man and the weight of a child, I gayly strode along. The first day I walked half a dozen miles at a very brisk pace, and came back without feeling in the least degree tired. These walks now became one of the greatest joys of my life. When nobody was looking, I would bound over a fence, sometimes just touching it with one hand, and sometimes not touching it at all. I delighted in rough places. I sprang over streams. I jumped and I ran. I felt like Mercury himself.

I now set about making another machine, so that my wife could accompany me in my walks; but when it was finished she positively refused to use it. "I can't wear a knapsack," she said, "and there is no other good way of fastening it to me. Besides, everybody about here knows I am no walker, and it would only set them talking."

I occasionally made use of this second machine, but I will only give one instance of its application. Some repairs were needed to the foundation-walls of my barn, and a two-horse wagon, loaded with building-stone, had been brought into my yard and left there. In the evening, when the men had gone away, I took my two machines and fastened them with strong chains, one on each side of the loaded wagon. Then, gradually turning the screws, the wagon was so lifted that its weight became very greatly diminished. We had an old donkey which used to belong to Herbert, and which was now occasionally used with a small cart to bring packages from the station. I went into the barn and put the harness on the little fellow, and, bringing him out to the wagon, I attached him to it. In this position he looked very funny, with a long pole sticking out in front of him and the great wagon behind him. When all was ready, I touched him up; and, to my great delight, he moved off with the two-horse load of stone as easily as if he were drawing his own cart. I led him out into the public road, along which he proceeded without difficulty. He was an opinionated little beast, and sometimes stopped, not liking the peculiar manner in which he was harnessed; but a touch of the switch made him move on, and I soon turned him and brought the wagon back into the yard. This determined the success of my invention in one of its most important uses, and with a satisfied heart I put the donkey into the stable and went into the house.

Our trip to Europe was made a few months after this, and was mainly on our son Herbert's account. He, poor fellow, was in great trouble, and so, therefore, were we. He had become engaged, with our full consent, to a young lady in our town, the daughter of a gentleman whom we esteemed very highly. Herbert was young to be engaged to be married, but as we felt that he would never find a girl to make him so good a wife, we were entirely satisfied, especially as it was agreed on all hands that the marriage was not to take place for some time. It seemed to us that in marrying Janet Gilbert, Herbert would secure for himself, in the very beginning of his career, the most important element of a happy life. But suddenly, without any reason that seemed to us justifiable, Mr. Gilbert, the only surviving parent of Janet, broke off the match; and he and his daughter soon after left the town for a trip to the West.

This blow nearly broke poor Herbert's heart. He gave up his professional studies and came home to us, and for a time we thought he would be seriously ill. Then we took him to Europe, and after a Continental tour of a month or two we left him, at his own request, in Göttingen, where he thought it would do him good to go to work again. Then we went down to the little town in Italy where my story first finds us. My wife had suffered much in mind and body on her son's account, and for this reason I was anxious that she should take outdoor exercise, and enjoy as much as possible the bracing air of the country. I had brought with me both my little machines. One was still in my knapsack, and the other I had fastened to the inside of an enormous family trunk. As one is obliged to pay for nearly every pound of his baggage on the Continent, this saved me a great deal of money. Everything heavy was packed into this great trunk,—books, papers, the bronze, iron, and marble relics we had picked up, and all the articles that usually weigh down a tourist's baggage. I screwed up the negative gravity apparatus until the trunk could be handled with great case by an ordinary porter. I could have made it weigh nothing at all, but this, of course, I did not wish to do. The lightness of my baggage, however, had occasioned some comment, and I had overheard remarks which were not altogether complimentary about people traveling around with empty trunks; but this only amused me.

Desirous that my wife should have the advantage of negative gravity while taking our walks, I had removed the machine from the trunk and fastened it inside of the basket, which she could carry under her arm. This assisted her wonderfully. When one arm was tired she put the basket under the other, and thus, with one hand on my arm, she could easily keep up with the free and buoyant steps my knapsack enabled me to take. She did not object to long tramps here, because nobody knew that she was not a walker, and she always carried some wine or other refreshment in the basket, not only because it was pleasant to have it with us, but because it seemed ridiculous to go about carrying an empty basket.

There were English-speaking people stopping at the hotel where we were, but they seemed more fond of driving than walking, and none of them offered to accompany us on our rambles, for which we were very glad. There was one man there, however, who was a great walker. He was an Englishman, a member of an Alpine Club, and generally went about dressed in a knickerbocker suit, with gray woolen stockings covering an enormous pair of calves. One evening this gentleman was talking to me and some others about the ascent of the Matterhorn, and I took occasion to deliver in pretty strong language my opinion upon such exploits. I declared them to be useless, foolhardy, and, if the climber had any one who loved him, wicked.

"Even if the weather should permit a view," I said, "what is that compared to the terrible risk to life? Under certain circumstances," I added (thinking of a kind of waistcoat I had some idea of making, which, set about with little negative gravity machines, all connected with a conveniently handled screw, would enable the wearer at times to dispense with his weight altogether), "such ascents might be divested of danger, and be quite admissible; but ordinarily they should be frowned upon by the intelligent public."

The Alpine Club man looked at me, especially regarding my somewhat slight figure and thinnish legs.

"It's all very well for you to talk that way," he said, "because it is easy to see that you are not up to that sort of thing."

"In conversations of this kind," I replied, "I never make personal allusions; but since you have chosen to do so, I feel inclined to invite you to walk with me to-morrow to the top of the mountain to the north of this town."

"I'll do it," he said, "at any time you choose to name." And as I left the room soon afterward I heard him laugh.

The next afternoon, about two o'clock, the Alpine Club man and myself set out for the mountain.

"What have you got in your knapsack?" he said.

"A hammer to use if I come across geological specimens, a field-glass, a flask of wine, and some other things."

"I wouldn't carry any weight, if I were you," he said.

"Oh, I don't mind it," I answered, and off we started.

The mountain to which we were bound was about two miles from the town. Its nearest side was steep, and in places almost precipitous, but it sloped away more gradually toward the north, and up that side a road led by devious windings to a village near the summit. It was not a very high mountain, but it would do for an afternoon's climb.

"I suppose you want to go up by the road," said my companion.

"Oh, no," I answered, "we won't go so far around as that. There is a path up this side, along which I have seen men driving their goats. I prefer to take that."

"All right, if you say so," he answered, with a smile; "but you'll find it pretty tough."

After a time he remarked:

"I wouldn't walk so fast, if I were you."

"Oh, I like to step along briskly," I said. And briskly on we went.

My wife had screwed up the machine in the knapsack more than usual, and walking seemed scarcely any effort at all. I carried a long alpenstock, and when we reached the mountain and began the ascent, I found that with the help of this and my knapsack I could go uphill at a wonderful rate. My companion had taken the lead, so as to show me how to climb. Making a *détour* over some rocks, I quickly passed him and went ahead. After that it was impossible for him to keep up with me. I ran up steep places, I cut off the windings of the path by lightly clambering over rocks, and even when I followed the beaten track my step was as rapid as if I had been walking on level ground.

"Look here!" shouted the Alpine Club man from below, "you'll kill yourself if you go at that rate! That's no way to climb mountains."

"It's my way!" I cried. And on I skipped.

Twenty minutes after I arrived at the summit, my companion joined me, puffing, and wiping his red face with his handkerchief.

"Confound it!" he cried, "I never came up a mountain so fast in my life."

"You need not have hurried," I said, coolly.

"I was afraid something would happen to you," he growled, "and I wanted to stop you. I never saw a person climb in such an utterly absurd way."

"I don't see why you should call it absurd," I said, smiling with an air of superiority. "I arrived here in a perfectly comfortable condition, neither heated nor wearied."

He made no answer, but walked off to a little distance, fanning himself with his hat and growling words which I did not catch. After a time I proposed to descend.

"You must be careful as you go down," he said.

"It is much more dangerous to go down steep places than to climb up."

"I am always prudent," I answered, and started in advance. I found the descent of the mountain much more pleasant than the ascent. It was positively exhilarating. I jumped from rocks and bluffs eight and ten feet in height, and touched the ground as gently as if I had stepped down but two feet. I ran down steep paths, and, with the aid of my alpenstock, stopped myself in an instant. I was careful to avoid dangerous places, but the runs and jumps I made were such as no man had ever made before upon that mountainside. Once only I heard my companion's voice.

"You'll break your —— neck!" he yelled.

"Never fear!" I called back, and soon left him far above.

When I reached the bottom I would have waited for him, but my activity had warmed me up, and as a cool evening breeze was beginning to blow I thought it better not to stop and take cold. Half an hour after my arrival at the hotel I came down to the court, cool, fresh, and dressed for dinner, and just in time to meet the Alpine man as he entered, hot, dusty, and growling.

"Excuse me for not waiting for you," I said; but without stopping to hear my reason, he muttered something about waiting in a place where no one would care to stay and passed into the house.

There was no doubt that what I had done gratified my pique and tickled my vanity.

"I think now," I said, when I related the matter to

my wife, "that he will scarcely say that I am not up to that sort of thing."

"I am not sure," she answered, "that it was exactly fair. He did not know how you were assisted."

"It was fair enough," I said. "He is enabled to climb well by the inherited vigor of his constitution and by his training. He did not tell me what methods of exercise he used to get those great muscles upon his legs. I am enabled to climb by the exercise of my intellect. My method is my business and his method is his business. It is all perfectly fair."

Still she persisted:

"He *thought* that you climbed with your legs, and not with your head."

And now, after this long digression, necessary to explain how a middle-aged couple of slight pedestrian ability, and loaded with a heavy knapsack and basket, should have started out on a rough walk and climb, fourteen miles in all, we will return to ourselves, standing on the little bluff and gazing out upon the sunset view. When the sky began to fade a little we turned from it and prepared to go back to the town.

"Where is the basket?" I said.

"I left it right here," answered my wife. "I unscrewed the machine and it lay perfectly flat."

"Did you afterward take out the bottles?" I asked, seeing them lying on the grass.

"Yes, I believe I did. I had to take out yours in order to get at mine."

"Then," said I, after looking all about the grassy patch on which we stood, "I am afraid you did not entirely unscrew the instrument, and that when the weight of the bottles was removed the basket gently rose into the air."

"It may be so," she said, lugubriously. "The basket was behind me as I drank my wine."

"I believe that is just what has happened," I said. "Look up there! I vow that is our basket!"

I pulled out my field-glass and directed it at a little speck high above our heads. It was the basket floating high in the air. I gave the glass to my wife to look, but she did not want to use it.

"What shall I do?" she cried. "I can't walk home without that basket. It's perfectly dreadful!" And she looked as if she was going to cry.

"Do not distress yourself," I said, although I was a good deal disturbed myself. "We shall get home very well. You shall put your hand on my shoulder, while I put my arm around you. Then you can screw up my machine a good deal higher, and it will support us both. In this way I am sure that we shall get on very well."

We carried out this plan, and managed to walk on with moderate comfort. To be sure, with the knapsack pulling me upward, and the weight of my wife pulling me down, the straps hurt me somewhat, which they had not done before. We did not spring lightly over the wall into the road, but, still clinging to each other, we clambered awkwardly over it. The road for the most part declined gently toward the town, and with moderate ease we made our way along it. But we walked much more slowly than we had done before, and it was quite dark when we reached our hotel. If it had not been for the light inside the court it would have been difficult for us to find it. A traveling-carriage was standing before the entrance, and against the light. It was necessary to pass around it, and my wife went first. I attempted to follow her, but, strange to say, there was nothing under my feet. I stepped vigorously, but only wagged my legs in the air. To my horror I found that I was rising in the air! I soon saw, by the light below me, that I was some fifteen feet from the ground. The carriage drove away, and in the darkness I was not noticed. Of course I knew what had happened. The instrument in my knapsack had been screwed up to such an intensity, in order to support both myself and my wife, that when her weight was removed the force of the negative gravity was sufficient to raise me from the ground. But I was glad to find that when I had risen to the height I have mentioned I did not go up any higher, but hung in the air, about on a level with the second tier of windows of the hotel.

I now began to try to reach the screw in my knapsack in order to reduce the force of the negative gravity; but, do what I would, I could not get my hand to it. The machine in the knapsack had been placed so as to support me in a well-balanced and comfortable way; and in doing this it had been impossible to set the screw so that I could reach it. But in a temporary arrangement of the kind this had not been considered necessary, as my wife always turned the screw for me until sufficient lifting-power had been attained.

I had intended, as I have said before, to construct a negative gravity waistcoat, in which the screw should be in front, and entirely under the wearer's control; but this was a thing of the future.

When I found that I could not turn the screw I began to be much alarmed. Here I was, dangling in the air, without any means of reaching the ground. I could not expect my wife to return to look for me, as she would naturally suppose I had stopped to speak to some one. I thought of loosening myself from the knapsack, but this would not do, for I should fall heavily, and either kill myself or break some of my bones. I did not dare to call for assistance, for if any of the simple-minded inhabitants of the town had discovered me floating in the air they would have taken me for a demon, and would probably have shot at me. A moderate breeze was blowing, and it wafted me gently down the street. If it had blown me against a tree I would have seized it, and have endeavored, so to speak, to climb down it; but there were no trees. There was a dim street lamp here and there, but reflectors above them threw their light upon the pavement, and none up to me. On many accounts I was glad that the night was so dark, for, much as I desired to get down, I wanted no one to see me in my strange position, which, to any one but myself and wife, would be utterly unaccountable. If I could rise as high as the roofs I might get on one of them, and, tearing off an armful of tiles, so load myself that I would be heavy enough to descend. But I did not rise to the eaves of any of the houses. If there had been a telegraph-pole, or anything of the kind that I could have clung to, I would have taken off the knapsack, and would have endeavored to scramble down as well as I could. But there was nothing I could cling to. Even the water-spouts, if I could have reached the face of the houses, were imbedded in the walls. At an open window, near which I was slowly blown, I saw two little boys going to bed by the light of a dim candle. I was dreadfully afraid that they would see me and raise an alarm. I actually came so near to the window that I threw out one foot and pushed against the wall with such force that I went nearly across the street. I thought I caught sight of a frightened look on the face of one of the boys; but of this I am not sure, and I heard no cries. I still floated, dangling, down the street. What was to be done? Should I call out? In that case, if I were not shot or stoned, my strange predicament, and the secret of my invention, would be exposed to the world. If I did not do this, I must either let myself drop and be killed or mangled, or hang there and die. When, during the course of the night, the air became more rarefied, I might rise higher and higher, perhaps to an altitude of one or two hundred feet. It would then be impossible for the people to reach me and get me down, even if they were convinced that I was not a demon. I should then expire, and when the birds of the air had eaten all of me that they could devour, I should forever hang above the unlucky town, a dangling skeleton, with a knapsack on its back.

Such thoughts were not re-assuring, and I determined

that if I could find no means of getting down without assistance, I would call out and run all risks; but so long as I could endure the tension of the straps I would hold out and hope for a tree or a pole. Perhaps it might rain, and my wet clothes would then become so heavy that I would descend as low as the top of a lamp-post.

As this thought was passing through my mind I saw a spark of light upon the street approaching me. I rightly imagined that it came from a tobacco-pipe, and presently I heard a voice. It was that of the Alpine Club man. Of all people in the world I did not want him to discover me, and I hung as motionless as possible. The man was speaking to another person who was walking with him.

"He is crazy beyond a doubt," said the Alpine man. "Nobody but a maniac could have gone up and down that mountain as he did! He hasn't any muscles, and one need only look at him to know that he couldn't do any climbing in a natural way. It is only the excitement of insanity that gives him strength."

The two now stopped almost under me, and the speaker continued:

"Such things are very common with maniacs. At times they acquire an unnatural strength which is perfectly wonderful. I have seen a little fellow struggle and fight so that four strong men could not hold him."

Then the other person spoke:

"I am afraid what you say is too true," he remarked. "Indeed, I have known it for some time."

At these words my breath almost stopped. It was

the voice of Mr. Gilbert, my townsman, and the father of Janet. It must have been he who had arrived in the traveling-carriage. He was acquainted with the Alpine Club man, and they were talking of me. Proper or improper, I listened with all my ears.

"It is a very sad case," Mr. Gilbert continued. "My daughter was engaged to marry his son, but I broke off the match. I could not have her marry the son of a lunatic, and there could be no doubt of his condition. He has been seen — a man of his age, and the head of a family — to load himself up with a heavy knapsack, which there was no earthly necessity for him to carry, and go skipping along the road for miles, vaulting over fences and jumping over rocks and ditches like a young calf or a colt. I myself saw a most heart-rending instance of how a kindly man's nature can be changed by the derangement of his intellect. I was at some distance from his house, but I plainly saw him harness a little donkey which he owns to a large two-horse wagon loaded with stone, and beat and lash the poor little beast until it drew the heavy load some distance along the public road. I would have remonstrated with him on this horrible cruelty, but he had the wagon back in his yard before I could reach him."

"Oh, there can be no doubt of his insanity," said the Alpine Club man, "and he oughtn't to be allowed to travel about in this way. Some day he will pitch his wife over a precipice just for the fun of seeing her shoot through the air."

"I am sorry he is here," said Mr. Gilbert, "for it

would be very painful to meet him. My daughter and I will retire very soon, and go away as early to-morrow morning as possible, so as to avoid seeing him."

And then they walked back to the hotel.

For a few moments I hung, utterly forgetful of my condition, and absorbed in the consideration of these revelations. One idea now filled my mind. Everything must be explained to Mr. Gilbert, even if it should be necessary to have him called to me, and for me to speak to him from the upper air.

Just then I saw something white approaching me along the road. My eyes had become accustomed to the darkness, and I perceived that it was an upturned face. I recognized the hurried gait, the form; it was my wife. As she came near me I called her name, and in the same breath entreated her not to scream. It must have been an effort for her to restrain herself, but she did it.

"You must help me to get down," I said, "without anybody seeing us."

"What shall I do?" she whispered.

"Try to catch hold of this string."

Taking a piece of twine from my pocket, I lowered one end to her. But it was too short; she could not reach it. I then tied my handkerchief to it, but still it was not long enough.

"I can get more string, or handkerchiefs," she whispered, hurriedly.

"No," I said; "you could not get them up to me. But, leaning against the hotel wall, on this side, in the corner, just inside of the garden gate, are some fishing-poles. I have seen them there every day. You can easily find them in the dark. Go, please, and bring me one of those."

The hotel was not far away, and in a few minutes my wife returned with a fishing-pole. She stood on tip-toe, and reached it high in air; but all she could do was to strike my feet and legs with it. My most frantic exertions did not enable me to get my hands low enough to touch it.

"Wait a minute," she said; and the rod was withdrawn.

I knew what she was doing. There was a hook and line attached to the pole, and with womanly dexterity she was fastening the hook to the extreme end of the rod. Soon she reached up, and gently struck at my legs. After a few attempts the hook caught in my trousers, a little below my right knee. Then there was a slight pull, a long scratch down my leg, and the hook was stopped by the top of my boot. Then came a steady downward pull, and I felt myself descending. Gently and firmly the rod was drawn down; carefully the lower end was kept free from the ground; and in a few moments my ankle was seized with a vigorous grasp. Then some one seemed to climb up me, my feet touched the ground, an arm was thrown around my neck, the hand of another arm was busy at the back of my knapsack, and I soon stood firmly in the road, entirely divested of negative gravity.

"Oh, that I should have forgotten," sobbed my wife, "and that I should have dropped your arms, and let you go up into the air! At first I thought that you had stopped below, and it was only a little while ago that the truth flashed upon me. Then I rushed out and began looking up for you. I knew that you had wax matches in your pocket, and hoped that you would keep on striking them, so that you would be seen."

"But I did not wish to be seen," I said, as we hurried to the hotel; "and I can never be sufficiently thankful that it was you who found me and brought me down. Do you know that it is Mr. Gilbert and his daughter who have just arrived? I must see him instantly. I will explain it all to you when I come upstairs."

I took off my knapsack and gave it to my wife, who carried it to our room, while I went to look for Mr. Gilbert. Fortunately I found him just as he was about to go up to his chamber. He took my offered hand, but looked at me sadly and gravely.

"Mr. Gilbert," I said, "I must speak to you in private. Let us step into this room. There is no one here."

"My friend," said Mr. Gilbert, "it will be much better to avoid discussing this subject. It is very painful to both of us, and no good can come from talking of it."

"You can not now comprehend what it is I want to say to you," I replied. "Come in here, and in a few minutes you will be very glad that you listened to me."

My manner was so earnest and impressive that Mr. Gilbert was constrained to follow me, and we went into a small room called the smoking-room, but in which people seldom smoked, and closed the door. I immediately began my statement. I told my old friend that I had discovered, by means that I need not explain at present, that he had considered me crazy, and that now the most important object of my life was to set myself right in his eyes. I thereupon gave him the whole history of my invention, and explained the reason of the actions that had appeared to him those of a lunatic. I said nothing about the little incident of that evening. That was a mere accident, and I did not care now to speak of it.

Mr. Gilbert listened to me very attentively.

"Your wife is here?" he asked, when I had finished.

"Yes," I said; "and she will corroborate my story in every item, and no one could ever suspect her of being crazy. I will go and bring her to you."

In a few minutes my wife was in the room, had shaken hands with Mr. Gilbert, and had been told of my suspected madness. She turned pale, but smiled.

"He did act like a crazy man," she said, "but I never supposed that anybody would think him one." And tears came into her eyes.

"And now, my dear," said I, "perhaps you will tell Mr. Gilbert how I did all this."

And then she told him the story that I had told.

Mr. Gilbert looked from the one to the other of us with a troubled air.

"Of course I do not doubt either of you, or rather I do not doubt that you believe what you say. All would be right if I could bring myself to credit that such a force as that you speak of can possibly exist."

"That is a matter," said I, "which I can easily prove to you by actual demonstration. If you can wait a short time, until my wife and I have had something to eat, — for I am nearly famished, and I am sure she must be, — I will set your mind at rest upon that point."

"I will wait here," said Mr. Gilbert, "and smoke a cigar. Don't hurry yourselves. I shall be glad to have some time to think about what you have told me."

When we had finished the dinner, which had been set aside for us, I went upstairs and got my knapsack, and we both joined Mr. Gilbert in the smoking-room. I showed him the little machine, and explained, very briefly, the principle of its construction. I did not give any practical demonstration of its action, because there were people walking about the corridor who might at any moment come into the room; but, looking out of the window, I saw that the night was much clearer. The wind had dissipated the clouds, and the stars were shining brightly.

"If you will come up the street with me," said I to Mr. Gilbert, "I will show you how this thing works."

"That is just what I want to see," he answered.

"I will go with you," said my wife, throwing a shawl over her head. And we started up the street.

When we were outside the little town I found the starlight was quite sufficient for my purpose. The white roadway, the low walls, and objects about us, could easily be distinguished.

"Now," said I to Mr. Gilbert, "I want to put this knapsack on you, and let you see how it feels, and how it will help you to walk." To this he assented with some eagerness, and I strapped it firmly on him. "I will now turn this screw," said I, "until you shall become lighter and lighter."

"Be very careful not to turn it too much," said my wife earnestly.

"Oh, you may depend on me for that," said I, turning the screw very gradually.

Mr. Gilbert was a stout man, and I was obliged to give the screw a good many turns.

"There seems to be considerable hoist in it," he said directly. And then I put my arms around him, and found that I could raise him from the ground. "Are you lifting me?" he exclaimed in surprise.

"Yes; I did it with ease," I answered.

"Upon — my — word!" ejaculated Mr. Gilbert.

I then gave the screw a half turn more, and told him to walk and run. He started off, at first slowly, then he made long strides, then he began to run, and then to skip and jump. It had been many years since Mr. Gilbert had skipped and jumped. No one was in sight, and he was free to gambol as much as he pleased. "Could you give it another turn?" said he, bounding up to me. "I want to try that wall." I put on a little more negative gravity, and he vaulted over a five-foot wall with great ease. In an instant he had leaped back into the road, and in two bounds was at my side. "I came down as light as a cat," he said. "There was never anything like it." And away he went up the road, taking steps at least eight feet long, leaving my wife and me laughing heartily at the preternatural agility of our stout friend. In a few minutes he was with us again. "Take it off," he said. "If I wear it any longer I shall want one myself, and then I shall be taken for a crazy man, and perhaps clapped into an asylum."

"Now," said I, as I turned back the screw before unstrapping the knapsack, "do you understand how I took long walks, and leaped and jumped; how I ran uphill and downhill, and how the little donkey drew the loaded wagon?"

"I understand it all," cried he. "I take back all I ever said or thought about you, my friend."

"And Herbert may marry Janet?" cried my wife.

"*May* marry her!" cried Mr. Gilbert. "Indeed he *shall* marry her, if I have anything to say about it! My poor girl has been drooping ever since I told her it could not be."

My wife rushed at him, but whether she embraced him or only shook his hands I can not say; for I had the knapsack in one hand, and was rubbing my eyes with the other.

"But, my dear fellow," said Mr. Gilbert directly, "if you still consider it to your interest to keep your invention a secret, I wish you had never made it. No one having a machine like that can help using it, and it is often quite as bad to be considered a maniac as to be one."

"My friend," I cried, with some excitement, "I have made up my mind on this subject. The little machine in this knapsack, which is the only one I now possess, has been a great pleasure to me. But I now know it has also been of the greatest injury indirectly to me and mine, not to mention some direct inconvenience and danger, which I will speak of another time. The secret lies with us three, and we will keep it. But the invention itself is too full of temptation and danger for any of us."

As I said this I held the knapsack with one hand while I quickly turned the screw with the other. In a few moments it was high above my head, while I with difficulty held it down by the straps. "Look!" I cried. And then I released my hold, and the knapsack shot into the air and disappeared into the upper gloom.

I was about to make a remark, but had no chance, for my wife threw herself upon my bosom, sobbing with joy.

"Oh, I am so glad — so glad!" she said. "And you will never make another?"

"Never another!" I answered.

"And now let us hurry in and see Janet," said my wife.

"You don't know how heavy and clumsy I feel," said Mr. Gilbert, striving to keep up with us as we walked back. "If I had worn that thing much longer, I should never have been willing to take it off!"

Janet had retired, but my wife went up to her room.

"I think she has felt it as much as our boy," she said, when she rejoined me. "But I tell you, my dear, I left a very happy girl in that little bed-chamber over the garden."

And there were three very happy elderly people talking together until quite late that evening. "I shall write to Herbert to-night," I said, when we separated, "and tell him to meet us all in Geneva. It will do the young man no harm if we interrupt his studies just now."

"You must let me add a postscript to the letter," said Mr. Gilbert, "and I am sure it will require no knapsack with a screw in the back to bring him quickly to us."

And it did not.

There is a wonderful pleasure in tripping over the earth like a winged Mercury, and in feeling one's self relieved of much of that attraction of gravitation which drags us down to earth, and gradually makes the movement of our bodies but weariness and labor. But this pleasure is not to be compared, I think, to that given by the buoyancy and lightness of two young and loving hearts, reunited after a separation which they had supposed would last for ever.

What became of the basket and the knapsack, or whether they ever met in upper air, I do not know. If they but float away and stay away from ken of mortal man, I shall be satisfied.

And whether or not the world will ever know more of the power of negative gravity depends entirely upon the disposition of my son Herbert, when — after a good many years, I hope — he shall open the packet my lawyers have in keeping.

[NOTE. — It would be quite useless for any one to interview my wife on this subject, for she has entirely forgotten how my machine was made. And as for Mr. Gilbert, he never knew.]

THE CLOVERFIELDS CARRIAGE.

NOT far from the roadside, in one of the southern counties of Virginia, there stood a neat log cabin, inhabited by a worthy negro couple, known as Uncle Elijah and Aunt Maria. These two had belonged to a widow lady, who owned the estate of Cloverfields, about three miles away; but when, a few years before the opening of our story, the close of the civil war had set them free, they, in common with nearly all the negroes in the county, thought it incumbent upon them, as an assertion of their independence, to leave their former owners, and either work for themselves or go into service elsewhere. Thus there was a general shifting from plantation to plantation. Uncle Elijah and his wife, both now past middle age, left the place where they had been born and raised, and hired this cabin on a neighboring plantation, where by day's labor and odd jobs on the part of the husband, and washing and ironing and chicken-raising on the part of the wife, they managed to live in moderate comfort.

Elijah had been the family coachman, and he had found it a hard thing to resign the dignity of this position; but had he retained it he would virtually have admitted to all his brethren and sisters that freedom had done nothing for him. In order to show that he was now director of his own fortunes, it was necessary that he should drop the reins by which he had so skillfully directed and controlled the two black carriage-horses which had been his especial care since their early colthood.

But his love for his old mistress and his sense of his former dignity never left him, and now, when from afar he saw approaching the familiar carriage, he would drop his work, or get up from his meal, and watch it until it had entirely disappeared from sight. Sometimes, if it were near enough, he would advance, hat in hand, to speak to his old mistress; but this he did not often do, — people might think he wanted to go back.

One autumn evening, just about dusk, as Uncle Elijah came out of his cabin, he perceived, near the top of a long hill on the road, the Cloverfields carriage and horses. Other eyes in the growing gloom might have not known what vehicle it was, but the eyes of Uncle Elijah could make no mistake. As he stood and gazed they sparkled with emotion.

"Whar Miss Jane gwine dis time o' night? An' wot's de matter wid dat kerridge!" he ejaculated. "I'll be dangdiddled ef de eberlastin' fool dat's dribin' hain't gwine an' chain' up de hin' wheel as ef it was a hay-wagin. An' who's de no' count idyit wot can't dribe down Red Hill widout chainin' de wheel? Lor'! how he do bump de stones! An' how dat mus' rile Miss Jane! But I reckin she mus' done got use' ter bein' riled, a pickin' up all sorts o' niggahs to dribe her kerridge."

When the vehicle reached the bottom of the hill, not far from the cabin, it stopped, and the driver got down to unchain the wheel. Possessed by a sudden thought, Uncle Elijah rushed into his house, from which his wife was happily absent, clapped on his hat, and seized his coat. Keeping well away from the road, he ran towards the carriage, climbed the fence, and approached the vehicle in the rear, where he would not be seen by any of its occupants. When he reached the man, who had just unfastened the chain, the soul of Uncle Elijah was filled with righteous indignation at finding it was Montague Braxton, a negro shoemaker of the neighborhood. Without a word he seized the cobbler coachman by the collar, including a good part of one ear in his grasp, and led him away from the carriage, Montague, who knew who had clutched him, submitting without a word. When they had hurriedly gone a dozen steps Elijah hissed in the other's ear:

"Is you comin' back ter-night?"

"Yaas," whispered the shoemaker, very much astonished at the manner of his interviewer.

"Well, den, jus' you go 'long up ter my house, split de wood fur Aun' M'riar, fotch a bucket ob water from de spring, and stay hyar till I come back. I'se gwine ter dribe dis kerridge myse'f. Ain't got no time to say no moh. Now, git!"

Montague, who knew "Uncle 'Lijah" as a pillar of strength in the church, as well as a pillar of not very easily restrained strength in his own proper person, made no answer, but noiselessly slipped away. Elijah passed quickly around the carriage, keeping at a little distance from it to avoid being recognized by those within, although he scarcely need have feared this in the dusky light, and mounted to the elevated seat in front; when, taking up the reins and whip, he started the horses, and the equipage moved on. Now sat Uncle Elijah like a king upon his throne, and his soul was moved within him with a joy that he had not known for years. Here were Gamma and Delta, the two horses that he had driven so long, a little older, a little browner in their manes and tails, but still the same good horses, with plenty of strength and spirit left; here was the same old harness — he could recognize it even in the dark — badly kept, and badly put on, but still the same; here were the reins that once no hand but his had ever dared to touch; and here the whip, very old now and shabby, with a miserable new lash on it, but still the same whip he used to wield; and here was the high seat on which he alone had sat from the time he became a man in years until that day when his freedom made him another man.

Now the thoughts of the regenerated coachman ran riot in his brain. Indignation towards the shoemaker who had dared to drive the family carriage of his old mistress on a night which promised to be as dark as this, first took entire possession of him.

"Dat no 'count cobbler!" he said to himself. "Wot he know 'bout dribin'? An' o' nights, too! An' wid de crick up. An' wid de water all ober de road 'longside for harf a mile. An' de road pas' Colonel

Tom Giles's all washed so dat he couldn't help slidin' inter de gully to sabe his soul, ef he hadn't fus' druv inter de crick, an' tumbled de kerridge an' hosses, an' his own eberlastin' fool se'f, top o' Miss Jane, an' mos' likely little Miss Jane an' Miss Almira Gay. But dey's all right now I'se dribin'. You ken bet your life on dat."

If any one had heard this remark, he would have been quite safe in accepting the wager, for, by day or by night, washed by rains, covered by freshets, or in their normal condition, Uncle Elijah knew the roads in this neighborhood better than any man alive, even since he had become a freeman he had studied the difficulties and obstructions of the highways as he walked to and from his work. "Ef I was a dribin' hyar," he would say to himself, "I'd put dis fron' wheel roun' dat little stone, den one small twis' ud bring de hin' wheel on dis side ob it, an' I'd clean miss de big rock in de udder rut."

Remembering and avoiding the stones, deep ruts, and encroaching gullies, Elijah, like a pilot who steers past the rocks and sandbars which lie under the water, as the road now lay in the darkness of the night, went steadily on, without bump or jolt of any account. Passing the flooded part of the road without deviating a foot to the right or left of the proper course, passing the tobacco field of Colonel Giles, where the rains had washed the road into a shelving hillside, without bumping an exposed rock or sliding towards a gully, he reached the higher and more level portion of the road, which was now so comparatively good and comparatively clear, to the sharp eyes of horses and driver, that Elijah went on at a fair pace, now and then waving his whip and straightening himself up as a man who breathes his native air once more. Suddenly a dreadful thought flashed across his mind, and he barely checked himself from pulling the horses back on their haunches.

"Whar's I gwine?" said he, almost aloud. "Dat double, eberlastin' fool shoemaker neber tole me! Whar kin Miss Jane, an' mos' like little Miss Jane an' Miss Almira Gay, be gwine at dis time? An' comin' back ter-night, too! Dey mus' be 'tendin' ter spen' de ebenin' somewhar, — but whar?"

Elijah now revolved in his mind every place to which he thought the family might be going. So far he had made no mistake because there had been no turn in the road; and although he had passed the place of Colonel Tom Giles, they could not be going to see him, for he was an old bachelor, living alone, and besides had gone to Richmond. A short distance ahead the road branched, and in one direction led to the house of Dr. Marshall Gordon, distant about a mile, and in the other to the hospitable mansion of General William Tucker.

"Dey can't be gwine fur de doctor fur anybody sick," thought Elijah, "fur if it had been dat dey'd sent a boy on a hoss, an' not hitched up de kerridge wid a shoemaker ter dribe; an' I'd be dreffel 'shamed ter take 'em more'n four miles to de Gin'ral's ef dey wasn't gwine dar."

The nearer he approached the fork of the road the more completely Uncle Elijah became convinced that he could not decide this important question for himself. It was absolutely necessary that he should get down and ask his old mistress where she was going. This was a terribly hard thing for him to do. He would be obliged to tell the whole story, and to admit that his affection for her, as strong as ever, had prompted him to take the driver's seat. And this was to relinquish a portion of his new freedom and manhood. But it had to be done, for the fork of the road was reached. Drawing up his horses, Elijah descended from his seat, and with the reins in one hand, for he was not a man, like the cobbler, to leave his horses standing free in the road, he reverently opened the carriage door.

"Miss Jane," said he, "I spec' you s'prised to see me dribin', but I couldn't stan' still an' let dat no 'count shoemaker, wot don' know nuffin 'bout hosses, nor de roads nuther, an' night comin' on pitch dark, dribe you. He hadn't eben sense 'nuf to tell me whar you's gwine, so I begs you'll scuse me fur gittin' down ter ax you."

They were now in the heavily shaded portion of the road, and the interior of the carriage was quite dark. From the farthest corner of the back seat came a thin, low voice which said to him: "Keep on now to the kyars."

This reply surprised Elijah in several ways. In the first place, he had confidently expected that his old mistress would say something expressive of her satisfaction in finding herself under his charge on such a dark night as this; and, again, he was surprised to hear that voice come out of the carriage. It did not belong to Miss Jane, nor, as far as he could judge, to any of her family. After a moment's hesitation he closed the door, and then, irresolutely, mounted to his seat and drove slowly on. He had not proceeded a hundred yards before there dawned upon his mind a dim recognition of the voice which had come from the carriage. Drawing up his horses again, he quickly got down and opened the carriage door.

"Who in dar, anyhow?" he said, in a tone by no means as respectful as that he had used before.

At this question the opposite door of the carriage suddenly opened, and the occupant popped out of it. As this individual, upon reaching the ground, turned, and stood facing Uncle Elijah, the latter could see, outlined upon a patch of sky behind him, the plainly discernible form of the cobbler, Montague, from whose lips now burst forth a roar of laughter that completely established his identity. The outraged soul of Uncle Elijah boiled and bubbled within him. He put out his left arm as if he would reach through the carriage and clutch the scoundrel by the throat. But this was impossible, and he would not drop the reins to run around the carriage.

"You eberlastin' fool cobbler!" he cried, "what fur you go play dis trick on me?"

"I no play no trick on you, Uncle 'Lijah," returned Montague, still laughing immoderately. "You played de trick on youse'f. I'se done nuffin but jus' keep out your way. I got up behin' so's ter see whar you was gwine, an' den I unhooked de back cuttins, an' slipped inside 'cause 'twas moh comf'ble."

"I'll break your neck fur dat!" cried Uncle Elijah. "A low-down, yaller shoemaker like you gittin' inter Miss Jane's kerridge!"

"Got ter ketch me fus', Uncle 'Lijah, 'fore you break my neck," replied the shoemaker, still in a merry mood.

"Shet up your fool talk!" cried Elijah, "an' tell me whar you was sent ter."

"I was sent fur Miss Polly Brown, de seamstress wot libes on Colonel Tom Giles's place, but dat was a long time back. She done gone ter bed afore dis. Miss Jane tole me ter go arly in the ebenin', but somebody done took one ob de hoss-collus fur de plow team, an' I couldn't find it nowhar, so it got right smart late afore I started. An' now you done tuck up so much time, Uncle 'Lijah, comin' way out hyar on your little business, dat 'tain't no use gwine fur Miss Polly Brown till de mawnin'. Whar *is* you gwine, anyhow, Uncle 'Lijah?"

To this Uncle Elijah made no answer, but his tone moderated a little as he asked: "Wot fur you tell me to keep on ter de kyars?"

"Cos I didn't know no udder place ter go, ef it was lef' ter me. 'Taint fur ter de kyars now, an' dar's allus sumfin dar fur de fam'ly, an' I'd ruther go back an' tell Miss Jane dat I done mistook whar she tole me ter go dan ter say I ain't been nowhar."

Uncle Elijah's mind was not a quick one, but it did not take a very long time for it to dawn upon him that in this predicament it might be better to go somewhere than nowhere. His anger had cooled down somewhat, for he felt that in his controversy with Montague he had had the worst of it. After rubbing the side of his head for a few moments he said shortly to the cobbler, "Shet dat doh', an' come 'long ter de kyars. Ef dar's anyt'ing dar fur de fam'ly, you kin git it, an' I'll dribe back. Aint gwine ter trus' you wid dese hosses in de night."

"Look hyar, Uncle 'Lijah," said Montague, coming round to the back of the carriage, but keeping well out of reach, "dar ain't gwine ter be no fitin' if I done git up 'longside o' you, is dar?"

"Come 'long hyar," said Uncle Elijah, mounting to his seat; "I ain't gwine ter fight while I got dese kerridge an' hosses under my chawge. But I don' say nuffin 'bout ter-morrer mawnin', min' dat."

"Don' keer nuffin' 'bout mawnin', long as 'tain't come," said Montague, getting up on the other side.

The railroad station was a little beyond Dr. Marshall Gordon's, and the road to it was one over which Elijah had gone so often that he felt warranted to drive at a good round pace, especially since he knew that his old mistress would not be bumped if he happened to strike a stone. His recollection of his previous careful driving made him grumble all the more at the shoemaker for having brought him on such a tom-fool errand.

"Now look hyar, Uncle 'Lijah," said Montague, "did you eber hear de par'ble ob de fox an' de mule?"

"Don' 'member no sich par'ble," said Elijah. "Is it in de Scripter?"

"I reckin so," said the shoemaker. "I neber read it dar myse'f but I spec's it's from de Scripter. Dar was a fox a-gwine ter de well fur a drink ob water, an' when he got dar he pull up de rope, an' sho' 'nuf dar wasn't no bucket to it. Dar had been a baptizin' at a church not fur off, an' as de baptizin' pond was all dried up, some ob de bredren come ter de well ter git some water, an' when dey saw dat de bucket was a good big one, dey t'ought dey mought as well take it 'long to baptize de sister right in it, cos she was a little chile on'y free weeks old."

"Dey don' dip 'em dat young," interrupted Elijah.

"Dis was a long time ago," said Montague, "an' a Mefodis' baby at dat. An' when de fox foun' out de bucket was gone, he jus' rar'd an' chawged, for he was pow'ful firsty, habin' bin eatin' fur his breakfus' some ob dat dar mean middlin' dat dey sen's up from Richmon', wot is moh salt dan meat. But sw'arin' wouldn't fotch de water up ter him, an' so he 'cluded ter climb down de rope, an' git a drink dat way. When he got down dar he drunk, an' he drunk, an' he drunk, an' when he felt mos' like fit to bus' he thought he'd had enuf, an' he'd go up ag'in. But when dat ole fox try ter climb up de rope, he fin' it right smart dif'rent wuk from comin' down, an' he couldn't git up nohow. When he foun' dis out he was pow'ful disgruntled, fur he had to stan' in de water, an' it was mighty cole, an' he 'spected he'd git de rheumatiz, an' have to have his legs wrop up in red flannel an' turpentine. While he was 'volvin' in his min' wot he'd do to dat sto'-keeper wot sole him dat salt middlin', 'long come a' army mule an' look down de well. He was p'intedly ole, dat mule, an' branded wid U.S. twice on bof sides, what had been guv to a preacher at Pow'tan Co'at House by de guv'ment, in de place ob a good mule dat de Yankees took."

"Th'ain't no mention of Pow'tan Co'at House in de Scripter," interrupted Elijah.

"Don' know 'bout dat," said Montague; "I reckin it's a Scripter name. Anyhow, de army mule he poke he head down de well, an' holler: 'Hello! Whar de bucket? an' who down dar?' 'Mawnin', Cap'n Mule,' said de fox. He was one ob dem red foxes dat ben hunt so offen by Gin'ral Tucker's pack of hounds dat it make him pow'ful peart. 'De bucket no 'count, Cap'n. De bottom's bruck out, an' it's been throwed away. Eberybody comes down de well arfter de water, an' I jus' tell you, Cap'n, it's mighty good dis mawnin'. Somebody mus' 'a' drop' a tickler an' a couple ob pounds ob sugar down hyar, fur it tastes jus' like apple toddy.' An' de fox he 'gan to lap wid he tongue as ef he could neber git enuf. When de army mule he heard 'bout de apple toddy, he say no moh, but jus' slid down de rope. 'Hello!' he holler when he git to de bottom. 'How you put your head down to drink? Th'ain't no room fur me ter put my head down.' 'Dat's so,' said de fox, who was scrouging ag'in' de wall to git out ob de way; 'you do fill up dis well 'mazin', an', sho' 'nuf, dar ain't no room fur you ter put your head down. But neber you min'. Jus' stan' still, an' I'll fix all dat.' De army mule, his hind legs was in de bottom ob de well, his forelegs was ag'in' de sides, an' he great long neck was stickin' eber so high up. Him gittin' right smart skeered 'bout dis time. De fox he jus' jump on de mule back, den on he neck, den on he head, an' den he gib one skip right out ob de well. 'Hello, dar!' hollered de mule. 'Whar you gwine? Come back hyar, an' haul me out dis well! What fur you go 'way an' leab me hyar?' De fox he come back, an' he look down de well, an' he say: 'Wot's de matter, mule?' An' de heart ob de mule went down into his hoofs when he notus he done lef' off de Cap'n. 'I got nuffin' ter do wid dat well, nur wid you nudder. Ef you wan' ter go down arfter apple toddy, dat's your look-out. Good-mawnin'.' An' off went Mr. Fox to de stoh' po'ch to tell the folks 'bout dat fool mule.

"Now that par'ble 'minds me ob you, Uncle 'Lijah. You didn't hab to git up on dis seat, an' hol' dese reins, an' dribe dese hosses, ef you hadn't wanted ter. 'Tain't no use jawin' me fur dat."

"Ef I wasn't 'feared dese hosses ud run away," roared Uncle Elijah, "I'd jus' take you down de road and give you sech a-hidin' as you haven't had sence you got inter breeches."

With Uncle Elijah's hands so fully occupied as they were, Montague felt safe; and, edging as near as possible to his end of the seat, he exclaimed:

"But dat ain't all de par'ble, Uncle 'Lijah. De fox he come back dat ebenin', an' when he looked down de well, dar de mule yit, sw'arin' an' cussin' like all out-doh's. When he see de fox, de mule he 'clar ter gracious dat when he git out he kick dat fox inter little bits so small dat they could sow him ober de fiel's from a wheat-seeder. 'Look hyar,' said de fox, 'you min' me ob de par'ble ob de man what los' his spring lamb. Somebody stole that lamb wot he 'spected to get foh' dollars fur at de Co'at House, an' de man he rar'd an' chawged, an' he swore dat ef he kotch dat t'ief he'd lick him wuss dan any sheep-t'ief was eber licked in dat county, or any ob de j'ining counties. He hunted high, an' he hunted low, to find de t'ief, an' jus' as he got inside de woods he come across a great big b'ar who had his spring lamb a hung up a-barbecuin', an' he was a-nailin' de skin up ag'in' a tree fur ter dry. De man was orful skeered; but de b'ar he sees him, an' he sings out: 'Hello! man, now you kotch de t'ief wot stole your spring lamb, why you no punch he head? Why you no break he back wid dat club? Tell me dat, you big man!' An' de b'ar he put down he hammer an' he nails so's ter talk de better. De man he too skeered to speak a word, an' he kep' squeezin' back, an' squeezin' back, widout sayin' nuffin'. De b'ar he come nigher an' nigher, an' he sing out: 'Wot fur you keep your mouf shut like a can o' temahters? Why you no do some ob dem big t'ings you blow 'bout jus' now?' De man he squeeze back, an' he squeeze back, till he git ter de edge ob de woods, and den he sing out: 'I mube dis meetin' 'journ! An' he more'n 'journed.

"Now, Uncle 'Lijah, I don' wan' ter make no 'flections 'gin' you in dis par'ble, but de fox he did say ter de mule dat 'fore he blow 'bout de big t'ings he gwine ter do, he better 'mune wid his own soul, an' see ef he able. Right smart fox dat, min' you, Uncle 'Lijah."

To this Uncle Elijah made no answer, but his eyes

sparkled, and his big hands were gripped very tightly on the whip and the reins that he held; and in a minute more he had drawn up at the little railroad station. Montague got down, and went to inquire if there were any packages of goods waiting for the Cloverfields family, while Elijah remained in his seat. This was a very familiar spot to the old negro. In former times he had been in the habit of driving here two or three times a week, and as he sat on his old seat on the carriage, with the same old reins in his hand, and the two black horses of the olden time again before him, and the familiar scenes all about him, Elijah actually forgot for the time being that he had ever resigned his ancient post.

"Look hyar," said Montague, presently returning with a package in his hands. "Hyar's some dry-goods from Richmon,' an' ef we hadn't druv down hyar, I'd been sent arfter 'em ter-morrer in de cart or on mule-back. De train's comin' in ten minutes; might as well wait, an' see ef dar's anythin' moh."

Elijah grumbled a little at waiting, but Montague, whose soul delighted in being stirred, even by so small a matter as the arrival of a railroad train, insisted that it would be unwise to go away, when a few minutes' delay might save a lot of future trouble. And so they waited.

Soon there was heard a distant whistle, then an approaching rumble, and the train rolled up to the station and stopped. As she had always done, Gamma tossed her head and looked to one side, while Delta pricked up his ears; but, as he had always done,

Uncle Elijah kept a firm hand upon the reins, and spoke to his horses in a low, quiet tone, which had the effect of making them understand that they might safely remain where they were, for under no circumstances would the train come their way.

Out of the open window of a car a young man put his head, and looked up and down the narrow platform, and then his eye was caught by the Cloverfields carriage, standing full in the light of the station lamp. Drawing in his head, he continued to look steadily at the carriage, and then he arose and came out on the car platform. One of the good comfortable stops, not unfrequent on the roads in this part of the country, was taking place, and the conductor had gone into the station to send a telegram. The young man came down to the bottom step, and again looked up and down. Here he was espied by Montague, who rushed up and accosted him.

"How d'ye, Mahs Chawles? Don' you 'member me? I'se Montague Braxton. Use' ter men' your boots."

"Isn't that Uncle Elijah?" asked the young man. "And who is the carriage waiting for?"

"Come fur you, sah," said the mendacious cobbler. "All ready waitin', sah. Gimme your checks, Mahs Chawles, an' I'll git de baggage."

"Come for me!" repeated the young man. "How did they know?"

"Cawn't tell nuffin' 'bout dat, sah, but Miss Jane she sen' me an' 'Lijah arfter you wid de kerridge. Better hurry up with de checks, sah."

The young man stood upon the bottom step looking steadily at the carriage, and paying no attention to Montague's last remark. Then he moved his eyes and saw the conductor coming out of the station. He turned, sprang up the steps and into the car, returning almost instantly with a valise and a light overcoat, which were immediately taken by the obsequious Montague.

"Dat all, sah?" said he.

The young man nodded. "All aboard!" cried the conductor. And in a moment the train had moved away.

Montague put the coat and valise on the front seat of the carriage, and stood holding open the door. "Hyar Mahs Chawles," said he to Elijah.

The old man turned so suddenly as to startle the horses. "Mahs Chawles!" he exclaimed, his eyes opening like a pair of head-lights.

"How d'ye, Uncle Elijah?" said the young man, extending his hand, which the old negro took as if he had been in a dream.

Montague looked a little anxiously at the two. "Better hurry up, sah," he said in a low voice. "It's gittin' late, an' Miss Jane's awful skeery 'bout dribin' at night."

At this the young man entered the carriage, Montague shut the door and ran around to his seat, and Uncle Elijah, his mind dazed and confused by this series of backward slides into times gone by, turned his horses and drove away. For ten minutes he spoke not a word, and then he said to Montague: "Did you know Mahs Chawles was comin'?"

"Ob course I did," said the cobbler. "You don' s'pose, Uncle 'Lijah, dat I'd fotch you all de way down hyar jus' fur a little bun'le ob cotton cloth? Didn't say nuffin' 'bout Mahs Chawles, cos I feared he mightn't come, an' you'd be dis'p'inted, an' dem par'bles was jus' ter pahs de time, Uncle 'Lijah — jus' ter pahs de time."

The old man made no answer, but drove steadily on, and the moon now having arisen, he was able to make very good time. Little more was said until they had nearly reached Uncle Elijah's cabin; then Montague asked the old man if he intended driving all the way to Cloverfields.

"Ob course I do," was the gruff reply. "You don' s'pose I'd trus' you wid Mahs Chawles dis time o' night?"

"Well, den," said the other, "I reckin I'll git down and cut acrost de fiel's ter my cabin ef you'll be 'bligin' enuf, Uncle 'Lijah, jes' ter put up de hosses when you gits dar, an' I'll come fus' t'ing in de mawnin' an' 'tend to eberyt'ing, jus' as I allus does."

"Go 'long," said Elijah, slackening his horses' pace. "I'se got no use fur you, nohow."

The mistress of Cloverfields, with little Miss Jane and Miss Almira Gay, was sitting in the parlor of the old mansion very much disturbed. In the middle of the afternoon Montague Braxton had been told to take the carriage and go for Miss Polly Brown, the seamstress, who had promised to give a week of her valuable time to Cloverfields; but, although it was now between nine and ten o'clock, he had not returned. The force of men-servants at Cloverfields was very small, and no one of them lived at the house excepting a very old man, too decrepit to send out to look up the lost cobbler and a carriage; and "Miss Jane," who was still a vigorous woman, though her hair was white, with her daughter, little Miss Jane, and her niece, Miss Almira Gay, had almost determined that they would walk over to a cabin about half a mile distant, and get a colored man living there to saddle a mule and ride to Miss Polly Brown's to see what had happened, when their deliberations were cut short by the sound of carriage-wheels on the drive. The three ladies sprang to their feet and hurried out to the porch, throwing the front door wide open that the light from the hall lamp might illumine the steps.

"Why, Miss Polly!" exclaimed little Miss Jane, what on earth——" And then she abruptly stopped, ejaculating in a low tone: "Uncle Elijah!"

At these words her mother moved quickly forward to the edge of the porch, but before she had time to say anything the carriage-door opened, and there stepped out, not the middle-aged seamstress who was expected, but a young man, on whose pale and upturned face the light of the hall lamp shone full. There was a cry from the women, a sudden bound up the steps, and in an instant the son of the house was in his mother's arms, with his sister clasping as much of his neck as she could reach.

A quarter of an hour after this, as Master Charles

sat in the parlor, his mother on one side with an arm around him, his sister on the other side with her arm around him, while his right hand clasped that of Miss Almira Gay, he thus explained himself: "I hadn't the least idea of getting off the train, for you know I had vowed never to come here till there was an end of that old trouble; but I thought if I went down to Danville in the late train we probably wouldn't stop at our station at all, and that I wouldn't notice when we passed it. But we did stop, and I couldn't help looking out, and when I saw the Cloverfields carriage standing there just as natural as life, and old Uncle Elijah in the driver's seat ——"

"Uncle Elijah!" exclaimed his mother, pushing back her chair. "Did he go down to the station to bring me my son?"

"It was Elijah!" cried little Miss Jane. "I saw him on the seat."

The old lady arose and left the room. She stepped upon the porch and looked out, but the carriage had gone. Then she went to the back door, hastily lighted a lantern which stood on the table, and with this in her hand made her way under the tall oaks and along the driveway to the barn, which was at some distance from the house. Through the open door of the stables she saw dimly the form of a man engaged in rubbing down a horse. Raising the lantern in her hand, she stepped to the door and threw the light within.

"Uncle Elijah," she said, "is that you?"

The man turned around. He forgot he had a vote; he forgot he could serve on a jury. He simply took off his hat, and coming forward, said: "Yaas, Miss Jane, dis is me."

The next morning, not very early, the cobbler approached the Cloverfields stables to attend to the horses, and to do the various oddments and bitments of work for which he had been temporarily hired. To his surprise, just as he turned a corner of the barn he met Uncle Elijah, who was engaged in attaching a new lash to the carriage-whip. Montague, astounded, stood for a moment speechless, gazing at Elijah, who, in some way, seemed to be different from what he was the day before. He looked taller and wider; his countenance was bright, his general aspect cheerful, and an element of Sunday seemed to have been infused into his clothes.

"Didn't spec' to see you hyar, Uncle 'Lijah," stammered the cobbler when he found his voice.

"Reckin not," said the old man, "but I'se glad ter see you, cos I wants ter tell you a par'ble. Dar was once a mud-turkle, de low-downest, or'nerest, no'countest mud-turkle in de whole worl'. His back was so cracked dat it wouldn't keep de rain off he skin, and he bottom shell bin ha'f sole' free or foh' times — he so lazy he ruther scuffle it ober de rocks dan walk — an' de chickens had eat off he tail afore de war, cos he too triflin' ter pull it in. Well, dis mis'ble mud-turkle come 'long one day, an' he sees a Chris'mus tukkey a-settin' on de limb ob a big apple-tree. De tukkey, he feel fus'-rate, an' he look fus'-rate, an' he jyin hese'f up dar 'mong de leabes an' de apples. An' de mud-turkle he look up, an' he say: 'Dat mighty nice up dar! Reckin I'd like ter set up dar myse'f. Jus' you come down, Mahs Chris'mus tukkey, an' lemme set up dar 'mongst de apples an' de leabes.' Den de Chris'mus tukkey, he bristle hese'f up, an' he stick out he feathers, an' he spread out he tail, an' his comb an' his gills git redder dan fire, an' he sing out: 'Go 'long wid you, you mud-turkle; don' lemme heah you say no moh 'bout settin' up hyar.' You dunno how to dribe a hoss; you got no moh sense dan ter chain de hin' wheel ob a kerridge, gwine down Red Hill; you lose de hoss-collus; you breaks de whip-lashes, and gits de harness all upside down wrong; an' you comes ter feed de hosses arfter dey's bin watered an' turned out moh'n two hours. P'raps you dunno who I is. I'se de driber ob de Cloverfields kerridge, an' as long as I has de use ob my j'ints, an' can see wid my eyes, nobody dribes dat kerridge but me. An' now, look hyar, you shoemaker mud-turkle, when me, an' Miss Jane, an' little Miss Jane, an' Miss Almira Gay, an' p'r'aps Mahs Chawles, gits ter de Happy Lan', don' you reckin dat you's gwine ter come dar too cos your foolin' helped fotch Mahs Chawles home. De angel Gabr'el, he p'int his horn right at you an' he sing out: 'Ain't got no use fur no yaller cobbler angels hyar, wid dey fool par'bles, an' dey lies 'bout bein' sent fur Mahs Chawles, an' dey lettin' Aun' M'riar split her own wood an' fotch her own water from de spring.' An' now you's got my par'ble, Montague Braxton, an' de nex' time you comes you gits your lickin'."

THE REMARKABLE WRECK OF THE "THOMAS HYKE."

IT was half-past one by the clock in the office of the Registrar of Woes. The room was empty, for it was Wednesday, and the Registrar always went home early on Wednesday afternoons. He had made that arrangement when he accepted the office. He was willing to serve his fellow-citizens in any suitable position to which he might be called, but he had private interests which could not be neglected. He belonged to his country, but there was a house in the country which belonged to him; and there were a great many things appertaining to that house which needed attention, especially in pleasant summer weather. It is true he was often absent on afternoons which did not fall on the Wednesday, but the fact of his having appointed a particular time for the furtherance of his outside interests so emphasized their importance that his associates in the office had no difficulty in understanding that affairs of such moment could not always be attended to in a single afternoon of the week.

But although the large room devoted to the especial use of the Registrar was unoccupied, there were other rooms connected with it which were not in that condition. With the suite of offices to the left we have nothing to do, but will confine our attention to a moderate-sized room to the right of the Registrar's office, and connected by a door, now closed, with that large and handsomely furnished chamber. This was the office of the Clerk of Shipwrecks, and it was at present occupied by five persons. One of these was the clerk himself, a man of goodly appearance, somewhere between twenty-five and forty-five years of age, and of a demeanor such as might be supposed to belong to one who had occupied a high position in state affairs, but who, by the cabals of his enemies, had been forced to resign the great operations of statesmanship which he had been directing, and who now stood, with a quite resigned air, pointing out to the populace the futile and disastrous efforts of the incompetent one who was endeavoring to fill his place. The Clerk of Shipwrecks had never fallen from such a position, having never occupied one, but he had acquired the demeanor referred to without going through the preliminary exercises.

Another occupant was a very young man, the personal clerk of the Registrar of Woes, who always closed all the doors of the office of that functionary on Wednesday afternoons, and at other times when outside interests demanded his principal's absence, after which he betook himself to the room of his friend the Shipwreck Clerk.

Then there was a middle-aged man named Mathers, also a friend of the clerk, and who was one of the eight who had made application for a sub-position in this department, which was now filled by a man who was expected to resign when a friend of his, a gentleman of influence in an interior county, should succeed in procuring the nomination as congressional representative of his district of an influential politician, whose election was considered assured in case certain expected action on the part of the administration should bring his party into power. The person now occupying the sub-position hoped then to get something better, and Mathers, consequently, was very willing, while waiting for the place, to visit the offices of the department and acquaint himself with its duties.

A fourth person was J. George Watts, a juryman by profession, who had brought with him his brother-in-law, a stranger in the city.

The Shipwreck Clerk had taken off his good coat, which he had worn to luncheon, and had replaced it by a lighter garment of linen, much bespattered with ink; and he now produced a cigar-box, containing six cigars.

"Gents," said he, "here is the fag end of a box of cigars. It's not like having the pick of the box, but they are all I have left."

Mr. Mathers, J. George Watts, and the brother-in-law each took a cigar with that careless yet deferential manner which always distinguishes the treatee from the treator; and then the box was protruded in an off-hand way toward Harry Covare, the personal clerk of the Registrar; but this young man declined, saying that he preferred cigarettes, a package of which he drew from his pocket. He had very often seen that cigar-box with a Havana brand, which he himself had brought from the other room after the Registrar had emptied it, passed around with six cigars, no more nor less, and he was wise enough to know that the Shipwreck Clerk did not expect to supply him with smoking material. If that gentleman had offered to the friends who generally dropped in on him on Wednesday afternoon the paper bag of cigars sold at five cents each when bought singly, but half a dozen for a quarter of a dollar, they would have been quite as thankfully received; but it better pleased his deprecative soul to put them in an empty cigar-box, and thus throw around them the halo of the presumption that ninety-four of their imported companions had been smoked.

The Shipwreck Clerk, having lighted a cigar for himself, sat down in his revolving chair, turned his back to his desk, and threw himself into an easy cross-legged attitude, which showed that he was perfectly at home in that office. Harry Covare mounted a high stool, while the visitors seated themselves in three wooden arm-chairs. But few words had been said, and each man had scarcely tossed his first tobacco ashes on the floor when some one wearing heavy boots was heard opening an outside door and entering the Registrar's room. Harry Covare jumped down from his stool, laid his half-smoked cigarette thereon, and bounced into the next room, closing the door after him. In about a minute he returned, and the Shipwreck Clerk looked at him inquiringly.

"An old cock in a pea-jacket," said Mr. Covare, taking up his cigarette, and mounting his stool. "I told him the Registrar would be here in the morning. He said he had something to report about a shipwreck; and I told him the Registrar would be here in the morning. Had to tell him that three times, and then he went."

"School don't keep Wednesday afternoons," said Mr. J. George Watts, with a knowing smile.

"No, sir," said the Shipwreck Clerk, emphatically, changing the crossing of his legs. "A man can't keep grinding on day in and out without breaking down. Outsiders may say what they please about it, but it can't be done. We've got to let up sometimes. People who do the work need the rest just as much as those who do the looking on."

"And more too, I should say," observed Mr. Mathers.

"Our little let-up on Wednesday afternoons," modestly observed Harry Covare, "is like death; it is sure to come, while the let-ups we get other days are more like the diseases which prevail in certain areas; you can't be sure whether you're going to get them or not."

The Shipwreck Clerk smiled benignantly at this remark, and the rest laughed. Mr. Mathers had heard it before, but he would not impair the pleasantness of his relations with a future colleague by hinting that he remembered it.

"He gets such ideas from his beastly statistics," said the Shipwreck Clerk.

"Which come pretty heavy on him sometimes, I expect," observed Mr. Mathers.

"They needn't," said the Shipwreck Clerk, "if things were managed here as they ought to be. If John J. Laylor," meaning thereby the Registrar, "was the right kind of a man, you'd see things very different here from what they are now. There'd be a larger force."

"That's so," said Mr. Mathers.

"And not only that, but there'd be better buildings, and more accommodations. Were any of you ever up to Anster? Well, take a run up there some day, and see what sort of buildings the department has there. William Q. Green is a very different man from John J. Laylor. You don't see him sitting in his chair and picking his teeth the whole winter, while the representative from his district never says a word about his department from one end of a session of Congress to the other. Now if I had charge of things here, I'd make such changes that you wouldn't know the place. I'd throw two rooms off here, and a corridor and entrance door at that end of the building. I'd close up this door," pointing toward the Registrar's room, "and if John J. Laylor wanted to come in here he might go round to the end door like other people."

The thought struck Harry Covare that in that case there would be no John J. Laylor, but he would not interrupt.

"And what is more," continued the Shipwreck Clerk, "I'd close up this whole department at twelve o'clock on Saturdays. The way things are managed now, a man has no time to attend to his own private business. Suppose I think of buying a piece of land, and want to go out and look at it, or suppose any one of you gentlemen were here and thought of buying a piece of land and wanted to go out and look at it, what are you going to do about it? You don't want to go on Sunday, and when are you going to go?"

Not one of the other gentlemen had ever thought of buying a piece of land, nor had they any reason to suppose that they ever would purchase an inch of soil unless they bought it in a flower-pot; but they all agreed that the way things were managed now there was no time for a man to attend to his own business.

"But you can't expect John J. Laylor to do anything," said the Shipwreck Clerk.

However, there was one thing which that gentleman always expected John J. Laylor to do. When the clerk was surrounded by a number of persons in hours of business, and when he had succeeded in impressing them with the importance of his functions, and the necessity of paying deferential attention to himself if they wished their business attended to, John J. Laylor would be sure to walk into the office and address the Shipwreck Clerk in such a manner as to let the people present know that he was a clerk and nothing else, and that he, the Registrar, was the head of that department. These humiliations the Shipwreck Clerk never forgot.

There was a little pause here, and then Mr. Mathers remarked:

"I should think you'd be awfully bored with the long

stories of shipwrecks that the people come and tell you."

He hoped to change the conversation, because, although he wished to remain on good terms with the subordinate officers, it was not desirable that he should be led to say much against John J. Laylor.

"No, sir," said the Shipwreck Clerk, "I am not bored. I did not come here to be bored, and as long as I have charge of this office I don't intend to be. The long-winded old salts who come here to report their wrecks never spin out their prosy yarns to me. The first thing I do is to let them know just what I want of them; and not an inch beyond that does a man of them go, at least while I am managing the business. There are times when John J. Laylor comes in, and puts in his oar, and wants to hear the whole story, which is pure stuff and nonsense, for John J. Laylor doesn't know anything more about a shipwreck than he does about——"

"The endemics in the Lake George area," suggested Harry Covare.

"Yes; or any other part of his business," said the Shipwreck Clerk; "and when he takes it into his head to interfere, all business stops till some second mate of a coal-schooner has told his whole story, from his sighting land on the morning of one day to his getting ashore on it on the afternoon of the next.— Now I don't put up with any such nonsense. There's no man living that can tell me anything about shipwrecks. I've never been to sea myself, but that's not necessary; and if I had gone, it's not likely I'd been wrecked. But I've read about every kind of shipwreck that ever happened. When I first came here I took care to post myself upon these matters, because I knew it would save trouble. I have read 'Robinson Crusoe,' 'The Wreck of the Grosvenor,' 'The Sinking of the Royal George,' and wrecks by waterspouts, tidal waves, and every other thing which would knock a ship into a cocked hat, and I've classified every sort of wreck under its proper head; and when I've found out to what class a wreck belongs, I know all about it. Now, when a man comes here to report a wreck, the first thing he has to do is just to shut down on his story, and to stand up square and answer a few questions that I put to him. In two minutes I know just what kind of shipwreck he's had; and then, when he gives me the name of his vessel, and one or two other points, he may go. I know all about that wreck, and I make a much better report of the business than he could have done if he'd stood here talking three days and three nights. The amount of money that's been saved to our tax-payers by the way I've systematized the business of this office is not to be calculated in figures."

The brother-in-law of J. George Watts knocked the ashes from the remnant of his cigar, looked contemplatively at the coal for a moment, and then remarked:

"I think you said there's no kind of shipwreck you don't know about?"

"That's what I said," replied the Shipwreck Clerk.

"I think," said the other, "I could tell you of a

shipwreck, in which I was concerned, that wouldn't go into any of your classes."

The Shipwreck Clerk threw away the end of his cigar, put both his hands into his trousers pockets, stretched out his legs, and looked steadfastly at the man who had made this unwarrantable remark. Then a pitying smile stole over his countenance, and he said: "Well, sir, I'd like to hear your account of it; and before you get a quarter through I can stop you just where you are, and go ahead and tell the rest of the story myself."

"That's so," said Harry Covare. "You'll see him do it just as sure pop as a spread rail bounces the engine."

"Well, then," said the brother-in-law of J. George Watts, "I'll tell it." And he began:

"It was just two years ago, the first of this month, that I sailed for South America in the "Thomas Hyke.""

At this point the Shipwreck Clerk turned and opened a large book at the letter T.

"That wreck wasn't reported here," said the other, "and you won't find it in your book."

"At Anster, perhaps?" said the Shipwreck Clerk, closing the volume, and turning round again.

"Can't say about that," replied the other. "I've never been to Anster, and haven't looked over their books."

"Well, you needn't want to," said the clerk. "They've got good accommodations at Anster, and the Registrar has some ideas of the duties of his post, but they have no such system of wreck reports as we have here."

"Very like," said the brother-in-law. And he went on with his story. "The 'Thomas Hyke' was a small iron steamer of six hundred tons, and she sailed from Ulford for Valparaiso with a cargo principally of pig iron."

"Pig iron for Valparaiso?" remarked the Shipwreck Clerk. And then he knitted his brows thoughtfully, and said, "Go on."

"She was a new vessel," continued the narrator, "and built with water-tight compartments; rather uncommon for a vessel of her class, but so she was. I am not a sailor, and don't know anything about ships. I went as passenger, and there was another one named William Anderson, and his son Sam, a boy about fifteen years old. We were all going to Valparaiso on business. I don't remember just how many days we were out, nor do I know just where we were, but it was somewhere off the coast of South America, when, one dark night, with a fog besides, for aught I know, for I was asleep, we ran into a steamer coming north. How we managed to do this, with room enough on both sides for all the ships in the world to pass, I don't know; but so it was. When I got on deck the other vessel had gone on, and we never saw anything more of her. Whether she sunk or got home is something I can't tell. But we pretty soon found that the 'Thomas Hyke' had some of the plates in her bow badly smashed, and she took in water like a thirsty dog. The captain had the forward water-tight bulkhead shut tight, and the pumps set to work, but it was no use. That forward compartment just filled up with water, and the 'Thomas Hyke' settled down with her bow clean under. Her deck was slanting forward like the side of a hill, and the propeller was lifted up so that it wouldn't have worked even if the engine had been kept going. The captain had the masts cut away, thinking this might bring her up some, but it didn't help much. There was a pretty heavy sea on, and the waves came rolling up the slant of the deck like the surf on the sea-shore. The captain gave orders to have all the hatches battened down so that water couldn't get in, and the only way by which anybody could go below was by the cabin door, which was far aft. This work of stopping up all openings in the deck was a dangerous business, for the decks sloped right down into the water, and if anybody had slipped, away he'd have gone into the ocean, with nothing to stop him; but the men made a line fast to themselves, and worked away with a good will, and soon got the deck and the house over the engine as tight as a bottle. The smoke-stack, which was well forward, had been broken down by a spar when the masts had been cut, and as the waves washed into the hole that it left, the captain had this plugged up with old sails, well fastened down. It was a dreadful thing to see the ship a-lying with her bows clean under water, and her stern sticking up. If it hadn't been for her water-tight compartments that were left uninjured, she would have gone down to the bottom as slick as a whistle. On the afternoon of the day after the collision the wind fell, and the sea soon became pretty smooth. The captain was quite sure that there would be no trouble about keeping afloat until some ship came along and took us off. Our flag was flying, upside down, from a pole in the stern; and if anybody saw a ship making such a guy of herself as the 'Thomas Hyke' was then doing, they'd be sure to come to see what was the matter with her, even if she had no flag of distress flying. We tried to make ourselves as comfortable as we could, but this wasn't easy with everything on such a dreadful slant. But that night we heard a rumbling and grinding noise down in the hold, and the slant seemed to get worse. Pretty soon the captain roused all hands, and told us that the cargo of pig iron was shifting and sliding down to the bow, and that it wouldn't be long before it would break through all the bulkheads, and then we'd fill and go to the bottom like a shot. He said we must all take to the boats, and get away as quick as we could. It was an easy matter launching the boats. They didn't lower them outside from the davits, but they just let 'em down on deck and slid 'em along forward into the water, and then held 'em there with a rope till everything was ready to start. They launched three boats, put plenty of provisions and water in 'em, and then everybody began to get aboard. But William Anderson, and me, and his son Sam, couldn't make up our minds to get into those boats and row out on the dark, wide ocean. They were the biggest boats we had, but still they were little things enough. The ship seemed to us to be a good deal safer, and more likely to be seen when day broke, than those three boats, which might be blown off if the wind rose, nobody knew where. It seemed to us that the cargo had done all the shifting it intended to, for the noise below had stopped; and, altogether, we agreed that we'd rather stick to the ship than go off in those boats. The captain, he tried to make us go, but we wouldn't do it; and he told us if we chose to stay behind and be drowned it was our affair, and he couldn't help it; and then he said there was a small boat aft, and we'd better launch her, and have her ready in case things should get worse, and we should make up our minds to leave the vessel. He and the rest then rowed off so as not to be caught in the vortex if the steamer went down, and we three stayed aboard. We launched the small boat in the way we'd seen the others launched, being careful to have ropes tied to us while we were doing it; and we put things aboard that we thought we should want. Then we went into the cabin, and waited for morning. It was a queer kind of a cabin, with a floor inclined like the roof of a house, but we sat down in the corners, and were glad to be there. The swinging lamp was burning, and it was a good deal more cheerful in there than it was outside. But, about daybreak, the grinding and rumbling down below began again, and the bow of the 'Thomas Hyke' kept going down more and more; and it wasn't long before the forward bulkhead of the cabin, which was what you might call its front wall when everything was all right, was under our feet, as level as a floor, and the lamp was lying close against the ceiling that it was hanging from. You may be sure that we thought it was time to get out of that. There were benches with arms to them fastened to the floor, and by these we climbed up to the foot of the cabin stairs, which, being turned bottom upward, we went down in order to get out. When we reached the cabin door we saw part of the deck below us, standing up like the side of a house that is built in the water, as they say the houses in Venice are. We had made our boat fast to the cabin door by a long line, and now we saw her floating quietly on the water, which was very smooth, and about twenty feet below us. We drew her up as close under us as we could, and then we let the boy Sam down by a rope, and after some kicking and swinging he got into her; and then he took the oars, and kept her right under us while we scrambled down by the ropes which we had used in getting her ready. As soon as we were in the boat we cut her rope and pulled away as hard as we could; and when we got to what we thought was a safe distance we stopped to look at the 'Thomas Hyke.' You never saw such a ship in all your born days. Two-thirds of the hull was sunk in the water, and she was standing straight up and down with the stern in the air, her rudder up as high as the topsail ought to be, and the screw propeller looking like the wheel on the top of one of these windmills that they have in the country for pumping up water. Her cargo had shifted so far forward that it had turned her right upon end, but she couldn't sink, owing to the air in the compartments that the water hadn't got into; and on the top of the whole thing was the distress flag flying from the pole which stuck out over the stern. It was broad daylight, but not a thing did we see of the other boats. We'd supposed that they wouldn't row very far, but would lay off at a safe distance until daylight; but they must have been scared and rowed farther than they intended. Well, sir, we staid in that boat all day, and watched the 'Thomas Hyke;' but she just kept as she was, and didn't seem to sink an inch. There was no use of rowing away, for we had no place to row to; and besides, we thought that passing ships would be much more likely to see that stern sticking high in the air than our little boat. We had enough to eat, and at night two of us slept while the other watched, dividing off the time, and taking turns to this. In the morning there was the 'Thomas Hyke' standing stern up just as before. There was a long swell on the ocean now, and she'd rise and lean over a little on each wave, but she'd come up again just as straight as before. That night passed as the last one had, and in the morning we found we'd drifted a good deal farther from the 'Thomas Hyke,' but she was floating just as she had been, like a big buoy that's moored over a sand-bar. We couldn't see a sign of the boats, and we about gave them up. We had our breakfast, which was a pretty poor meal, being nothing but hard-tack and what was left of a piece of boiled beef. After we'd sat for a while doing nothing, but feeling mighty uncomfortable, William Anderson said: 'Look here, do you know that I think we would be three fools to keep on shivering all night and living on hard-tack in the day-time, when there's plenty on that vessel for us to eat, and to keep us warm. If she's floated that way for two days and two nights, there's no knowing how much longer she'll float, and we might as well go on board and get the things we want as not.' 'All right,' said I, for I was tired doing nothing, and Sam was as willing as anybody. So we rowed up to the steamer, and stopped close to the deck, which, as I said before, was standing straight up out of the water like the wall of a house. The cabin door, which was the only opening into her, was about twenty feet above us, and the ropes which we had tied to the rails of the stairs inside were still hanging down. Sam was an active youngster, and he managed to climb up one of these ropes; but when he got to the door he drew it up and tied knots in it about a foot apart, and then he let it down to us, for neither William Anderson nor me could go up a rope hand over hand without knots or something to hold on to. As it was, we had a lot of bother getting up, but we did it at last, and then we walked up the stairs, treading on the front part of each step instead of the top of it, as we would have done if the stairs had been in their proper position. When we got to the floor of the cabin, which was now perpendicular like a wall, we had to clamber down by means of the furniture, which was screwed fast, until we reached the bulkhead, which was now the floor of the cabin. Close to this bulkhead was a small room which was the steward's pantry, and here we found lots of things to eat, but all jumbled up in a way that made us laugh. The boxes of biscuits and the tin cans, and a lot of bottles in wicker covers, were piled up on one end of the room, and everything in the lockers and drawers was jumbled together. William Anderson and me set to work to get out what we thought we'd want, and we told Sam to climb up into some of the state-rooms, of which there were four on each side of the cabin, and get some blankets to keep us warm, as well as a few sheets, which we thought we could rig up for an awning to the boat; for the days were just as hot as the nights were cool. When we'd collected what we wanted, William Anderson and me climbed into our own rooms, thinking we'd each pack a valise with what we most wanted to save of our clothes and things; and while we were doing this, Sam called out to us that it was raining. He was sitting at the cabin door looking out. I first thought to tell him to shut the door so's to keep the rain from coming in; but when I thought how things really were, I laughed at the idea. There was a sort of little house built over the entrance to the cabin, and in one end of it was the door; and in the way the ship now was the open doorway was underneath the little house, and of course no rain could come in. Pretty soon we heard the rain pouring down, beating on the stern of the vessel like hail. We got to the stairs and looked out. The rain was falling in perfect sheets, in a way you never see except round about the tropics. 'It's a good thing we're inside,' said William Anderson, 'for if we'd been out in this rain we'd been drowned in the boat.' I agreed with him, and we made up our minds to stay where we were until the rain was over. Well, it rained about four hours; and when it stopped, and we looked out, we saw our little boat nearly full of water, and sunk so deep that if one of us had stepped on her she'd have gone down, sure. 'Here's a pretty kittle of fish,' said William Anderson; 'there's nothing for us to do now but to stay where we are.' I believe in his heart he was glad of that, for if ever a man was tired of a little boat, William Anderson was tired of that one we'd been in for two days and two nights. At any rate there was no use talking about it, and we set to work to make ourselves comfortable. We got some mattresses and pillows out of the staterooms, and when it began to get dark we lighted the lamp, which we had filled with sweet-oil from a flask in the pantry, not finding any other kind, and we hung it from the railing of the stairs. We had a good night's rest, and the only thing that disturbed me was William Anderson lifting up his head every time he turned over, and saying how much better this was than that blasted little boat. The next morning we had a good breakfast, even making some tea with a spirit lamp we found, using brandy instead of alcohol. William Anderson and I wanted to get into the captain's room, which was near the stern, and pretty high up, so as to see if there was anything there that we ought to get ready to save when a vessel should come along and pick us up; but we were not good at climbing, like Sam, and we didn't see how we could get up there. Sam said he was sure he had once seen a ladder in the compartment just forward of the bulkhead, and as William was very anxious to get up to the captain's room, we let the boy go and look for it. There was a sliding door in the bulkhead under our feet, and we opened this far enough to let Sam get through; and he scrambled down like a monkey into the next compartment, which was light enough, although the lower half of it, which was next to the engine-room, was under the water-line. Sam actually found a ladder with hooks at one end of it, and while he was handing it up to us, which was very hard to do, for he had to climb up on all sorts of things, he let it topple over, and the end with the iron hooks fell against the round glass of one of the port-holes. The glass was very thick and strong, but the ladder came down very heavy and shivered it. As bad luck would have it, this window was below the water-line, and the water came rushing in in a big spout. We chucked blankets down to Sam for him to stop up the hole, but 'twas of no use; for it was hard for him to get at the window, and when he did the water came in with such force that he couldn't get a blanket into the hole. We were afraid he'd be drowned down there, and told him to come out as quick as he could. He put up the ladder again, and hooked it on to the door in the bulkhead, and we held it while he climbed up. Looking down through the doorway, we saw, by the way the water was pouring in at the opening, that it wouldn't be long before that compartment was filled up; so we shoved the door to and made it all tight, and then said William Anderson: 'The ship'll sink deeper and deeper as that fills up, and the water may get up to the cabin door, and we must go and make that as tight as we can.' Sam had pulled the ladder up after him, and this we found of great use in getting to the foot of the cabin stairs. We shut the cabin door, and locked and bolted it; and as it fitted pretty tight, we didn't think it would let in much water if the ship sunk that far. But over the top of the cabin stairs were a couple of folding doors, which shut down horizontally when the ship was in its proper position, and which were only used in very bad, cold weather. These we pulled to and fastened tight, thus having a double protection against the water. Well, we didn't get this done any too soon, for the water did come up to the cabin door, and a little trickled in from the outside door, and through the cracks in the inner one. But we went to work and stopped these up with strips from the sheets, which we crammed well in with our pocket knives. Then we sat down on the steps, and waited to see what would happen next. The doors of all the state-rooms were open, and we could see through the thick plate-glass windows in them, which were all shut tight, that the ship was sinking more and more as the water came in. Sam climbed up into one of the after state-rooms, and said the outside water was nearly up to the stern; and pretty soon we looked up to the two port-holes in the stern, and saw that they were covered with water; and as more and more water could be seen there, and as the light came through less easily, we knew that we were sinking under the surface of the ocean. 'It's a mighty good thing,' said William Anderson, 'that no water can get in here.' William had a hopeful kind of mind, and always looked on the bright side of things; but I must say that I was dreadfully scared when I looked through those stern windows and saw water instead of sky. It began to get duskier and duskier as we sank lower and lower, but still we could see pretty well, for it's astonishing how much light comes down through water. After a little while we noticed that the light remained about the same; and then William Anderson he sings out: 'Hooray, we've stopped sinking!' 'What difference does that make?' says I. 'We must be thirty or forty feet under water, and more yet for aught I know.' 'Yes, that may be,' said he; 'but it is clear that all the water has got into that compartment that can get in, and we have sunk just as far down as we are going.' 'But that don't help matters,' said I; 'thirty or forty feet under water is just as bad as a thousand as to drowning a man.' 'Drowning!' said William; 'how are you going to be drowned? No water can get in here.' 'Nor no air, either,' said I; 'and people are drowned for want of air, as I take it.' 'It would be a queer sort of thing,' said William, 'to be drowned in the ocean and yet stay as dry as a chip. But it's no use being worried about air. We've got air enough here to last us for ever so long. This stern compartment is the biggest in the ship, and it's got lots of air in it. Just think of that hold! It must be nearly full of air. The stern compartment of the hold has got nothing in it but sewing-machines. I saw 'em loading her. The pig-iron was mostly amidships, or at least forward of this compartment. Now, there's no kind of a cargo that'll accommodate as much air as sewing-machines. They're packed in wooden frames, not boxes, and don't fill up half the room they take. There's air all through and around 'em. It's a very comforting thing to think the hold isn't filled up solid with bales of cotton or wheat in bulk.' It might be comforting, but I couldn't get much good out of it. And now Sam, who'd been scrambling all over the cabin to see how things were going on, sung out that the water was leaking in a little again at the cabin door, and around some of the iron frames of the windows. ' It's a lucky thing,' said William Anderson, ' that we didn't sink any deeper, or the pressure of the water would have burst in those heavy glasses. And what we've got to do now is to stop up all the cracks. The more we work, the livelier we'll feel.' We tore off more strips of sheets and went all round, stopping up cracks wherever we found them. ' It's fortunate,' said William Anderson, ' that Sam found that ladder, for we would have had hard work getting to the windows of the stern state-rooms without it; but by resting it on the bottom step of the stairs, which now happens to be the top one, we can get to any part of the cabin.' I couldn't help thinking that if Sam hadn't found the ladder it would have been a good deal better for us; but I didn't want to damp William's spirits, and I said nothing.

"And now I beg your pardon, sir," said the narrator, addressing the Shipwreck Clerk, "but I forgot that you said you'd finish this story yourself. Perhaps you'd like to take it up just here?"

The Shipwreck Clerk seemed surprised, and had, apparently, forgotten his previous offer. "Oh, no," said he, " tell your own story. This is not a matter of business."

"Very well, then," said the brother-in-law of J. George Watts, "I'll go on. We made everything as tight as we could, and then we got our supper, having forgotten all about dinner, and being very hungry. We didn't make any tea, and we didn't light the lamp, for we knew that would use up air; but we made a better meal than three people sunk out of sight in the ocean had a right to expect. 'What troubles me most,' said William Anderson, as he turned in, 'is the fact that if we are forty feet under water, our flag-pole must be covered up. Now, if the flag was sticking out, upside down, a ship sailing by would see it and would know there was something wrong.' 'If that's all that troubles you,' said I, 'I guess you'll sleep easy. And if a ship was to see the flag, I wonder how they'd know we were down here, and how they'd get us out if they did!' 'Oh, they'd manage it,' said William Anderson; 'Trust those sea-captains for that.' And then he went to sleep. The next morning the air began to get mighty disagreeable in the part of the cabin where we were, and then William Anderson he says: 'What we've got to do is to climb up into the stern state-rooms, where the air is purer. We can come down here to get our meals, and then go up again to breathe comfortable.' 'And what are we going to do when the air up there gets foul?' says I to William, who seemed to be making arrangements for spending the summer in our present quarters. 'Oh, that'll be all right,' said he. 'It don't do to be extravagant with air any more than with anything else. When we've used up all there is in this cabin, we can bore holes through the floor into the hold and let in air from there. If we're economical, there'll be enough to last for dear knows how long.' We passed the night each in a state-room, sleeping on the end wall instead of the berth, and it wasn't till the afternoon of the next day that the air of the cabin got so bad we thought we'd have some fresh; so we went down on the bulkhead, and with an auger that we found in the pantry we bored three holes, about a yard apart, in the cabin floor, which was now one of the walls of the room, just as the bulkhead was the floor, and the stern end, where the two round windows were, was the ceiling or roof. We each took a hole, and I tell you it was pleasant to breathe the air which came in from the hold. 'Isn't this jolly?' said William Anderson. 'And we ought to be mighty glad that that hold wasn't loaded with codfish or soap. But there's nothing that smells better than new sewing-machines that haven't ever been used, and this air is pleasant enough for anybody.' By William's advice we made three plugs, by which we stopped up the holes when we thought we'd had air enough for the present. 'And now,' says he, 'we needn't climb up into those awkward state-rooms any more. We can just stay down here and be comfortable, and let in air when we want it.' 'And how long do you suppose that air in the hold is going to last?' said I. 'Oh, ever so long,' said he, 'using it so economically as we do; and when it stops coming out lively through these little holes, as I suppose it will after a while, we can saw a big hole in this flooring and go into the hold, and do our breathing, if we want to.' That evening we did saw a hole about a foot square, so as to have plenty of air while we were asleep, but we didn't go into the hold, it being pretty well filled up with machines; though the next day Sam and I sometimes stuck our heads in for a good sniff of air, though William Anderson was opposed to this, being of the opinion that we ought to put ourselves on short rations of breathing so as to make the supply of air hold out as long as possible. 'But what's the good,' said I to William, 'of trying to make the air hold out if we've got to be suffocated in this place after all?' 'What's the good?' says he. 'Haven't you enough biscuits, and canned meats, and plenty of other things to eat, and a barrel of water in that room opposite the pantry, not to speak of wine and brandy if you want to cheer yourself up a bit, and haven't we good mattresses to sleep on, and why shouldn't we try to live and be comfortable as long as we can?' 'What I want,' said I, 'is to get out of this box. The idea of being shut up in here down under the water is more than I can stand. I'd rather take my chances going up to the surface and swimming about till I found a piece of the wreck, or something to float on.' 'You needn't think of anything of that sort,' said William, ' for if we were to open a door or a window to get out, the water'd rush in and drive us back and fill up this place in no time; and then the whole concern would go to the bottom. And what would you do if you did get to the top of the water? It's not likely you'd find anything there to get on, and if you did you wouldn't live very long floating about with nothing to eat. No, sir,' says he, ' what we've got to do is to be content with the comforts we have around us, and something will turn up to get us out of this; you see if it don't.' There was no use talking against William Anderson, and I didn't say any more about getting out. As for Sam, he spent his time at the windows of the state-rooms a-looking out. We could see a good way into the water, further than you would think, and we sometimes saw fishes, especially porpoises, swimming about, most likely trying to find out what a ship was doing hanging bows down under the water. What troubled Sam was that a sword-fish might come along and jab his sword through one of the windows. In that case it would be all up, or rather down, with us. Every now and then he'd sing out, ' Here comes one!' And then, just as I'd give a jump, he'd say, ' No, it isn't; it's a porpoise.' I thought from the first, and I think now, that it would have been a great deal better for us if that boy hadn't been along. That night there was a good deal of motion to the ship, and she swung about and rose up and down more than she had done since we'd been left in her. ' There must be a big sea running on top,' said William Anderson, ' and if we were up there we'd be tossed about dreadful. Now the motion down here is just as easy as a cradle, and, what's more, we can't be sunk very deep; for if we were, there wouldn't be any motion at all.' About noon the next day we felt a sudden tremble and shake run through the whole ship, and far down under us we heard a rumbling and grinding that nearly scared me out of my wits. I first thought we'd struck bottom, but William he said that couldn't be, for it was just as light in the cabin as it had been, and if we'd gone down it would have grown much darker, of course. The rumbling stopped after a little while, and then it seemed to grow lighter instead of darker; and Sam, who was looking up at the stern windows over our heads, he sung out, 'Sky!' And, sure enough, we could see the blue sky, as clear as daylight, through those windows! And then the ship, she turned herself on the slant, pretty much as she had been when her forward compartment first took in water, and we found ourselves standing on the cabin floor instead of the bulkhead. I was near one of the open state-rooms, and as I looked in there was the sunlight coming through the wet glass in the window, and more cheerful than anything I ever saw before in this world. William Anderson he just made one jump, and, unscrewing one of the state-room windows, he jerked it open. We had thought the air inside was good enough to last some time longer; but when that window was open and the fresh air came rushing in, it was a different sort of thing, I can tell you. William put his head out and looked up and down and all around. 'She's nearly all out of water!' he shouted, 'and we can open the cabin door.' Then we all three rushed at those stairs, which were nearly right side up now, and we had the cabin doors open in no time. When we looked out we saw that the ship was truly floating pretty much as she had been when the captain and crew left her, though we all agreed that her deck didn't slant as much forward as it did then. 'Do you know what's happened?' sung out William Anderson, after he'd stood still for a minute to look around and think. 'That bobbing up and down that the vessel got last night shook up and settled down the pig-iron inside of her, and the iron plates in the bow, that were smashed and loosened by the collision, have given way under the weight, and the whole cargo of pig-iron has burst through and gone to the bottom. Then, of course, up we came. Didn't I tell you something would happen to make us all right?'

"Well, I won't make this story any longer than I can help. The next day after that we were taken off by a sugar-ship bound north, and we were carried safe back to Ulford, where we found our captain and the crew, who had been picked up by a ship after they'd been three or four days in their boats. This ship had sailed our way to find us, which, of course, she couldn't do, as at that time we were under water and out of sight.

"And now, sir," said the brother-in-law of J. George Watts to the Shipwreck Clerk, "to which of your classes does this wreck of mine belong?"

"Gents," said the Shipwreck Clerk, rising from his seat, "it's four o'clock, and at that hour this office closes."

MY BULL-CALF.

I AM an animal painter, and although I am not well known to fame, I have painted a good many pictures, most of which may now be seen on the walls of my studio. In justice to myself I must say that the critics of the art exhibitions and those persons competent to judge who have visited my studio have spoken in praise of my pictures, and have given me a good place among the younger artists of the country; sometimes, indeed, they have said things about the suggested sentiment of some of my work which I am too modest here to repeat. But in spite of this commendation, which I labor hard to deserve, there has been no great demand for my paintings.

A facetious brother artist once attempted to explain the slowness of my sales. "You see," said he, "that painting changes the nature of its subjects. In real life animals frequently go off very rapidly, but when they are painted they don't."

The same gentleman also made a good deal of fun of one of my first paintings — a dead lion. This animal had died in a menagerie in the city, and having heard of his decease, I bought his remains for five dollars, and after dark I conveyed them to my studio in a wheelbarrow. I was quite young and enthusiastic then, and as the animal had apparently died of a consumption, he was not very heavy. I worked day and night at a life-size (so to speak) portrait of the beast, and it was agreed by all who saw it that I succeeded very well. But no one seemed inclined in the slightest degree to buy the picture. "What you are waiting for," said my facetious friend, " is the visit of a live ass. When he comes along he will buy that thing, and make your fortune."

My latest work was a life-size picture of a bull-calf. Some time before, I determined to devote myself to cattle painting, and had bought a cow for a model. This I did because I found it difficult to have control over the cows of other people. I live a short distance out of town, and while the farmers thereabout were very willing that I should go into the field and sketch their cows, they would not allow me to pen one of them up in a confined space where I could study her form and features without following her, easel and material in hand, over a wide and sometimes marshy pasture. My cow proved a very valuable possession. I rented a small grassy field for her, and put up a cheap and comfortable shed in one corner of it. I sold her milk to the good lady with whom I lived, and my model cow paid all her expenses, attendance included. She was a gentle creature, and becoming accustomed to my presence, would generally remain in one position for a long time, and when I stirred her up would readily assume some other attitude of repose. I did not always copy her exactly. Sometimes I gave her one color and sometimes another, and sometimes several blended; at one time I gave her horns, and at another none; and in this way I frequently made a herd of her, scattering her over a verdant mead. I did not always even paint her as a cow. With a different head and branching horns, a longer neck, a thinner body, a shorter tail, and longer legs, she made an excellent stag, the life-like poses which I was enabled to get giving the real value to the picture. Once I painted her as a sphinx, her body couched in the conventional way, with claws at the ends of the legs instead of hoofs, and a little altered in contour, making an admirable study; and there was an expression in her eye, as she meditatively crunched a cabbage leaf, which made me give it to the woman's head that I placed upon her.

"What a far-off, prophetic look it has!" said one who stood before the picture when it was finished. "It seems to gaze across the sands of Egypt, and to see things thousands of years ahead. If you could fix up a little bit of sunset in the distance, with some red and yellow clouds in the shape of the flag of England, the symbolized sentiment would be quite perfect."

The bull-calf which afterward served as my model was the son of my cow. When he was old enough to go about by himself and eat hay and grass, I sold his mother at a good profit, and retained him as a model, and the life-size picture of him, on which I worked for a long time, was my masterpiece. When it was nearly finished I brought it to my studio, and there day after day I touched and retouched it, often thinking it finished, but always finding, when I went home and looked at my calf, that there was something of life and truth in the real animal which I had not given to the picture, and which I afterward strove to suggest, if not to copy.

I had a friend who occupied a studio in the same building, and who took a great interest in the portrait of my bull-calf. The specialty of this artist was quiet landscape and flowers, and we had frequently gone into the country and sketched together, the one drawing the cattle, and the other the field in which they roved. One day we stood before my almost completed work.

"What a spirited and life-like air he has!" remarked my companion. "He looks as if he was just about to hunch up his back, give a couple of awkward skips, and then butt at us. I really feel like shutting the door, when I come in, for fear he should jump down and run away. You are going to brighten up the foreground a little, are you not?"

"Yes," I answered; "and what it needs is a modest cluster of daisies in this corner. Won't you paint them in for me? You can do it so much better than I can!"

"No," she answered; "I positively will not. No one but yourself should touch it. It is your very best work, and it should be all your picture."

In the course of my life I had not had, or at least I believed that I had not had, many of those pieces of good fortune which people call "opportunities."

Now here was one, and I determined to seize it. "Why can it not be *our* picture?" I asked.

She looked up at me with a quick glance, which seemed to say, "What! are you about to speak at last?"

In ten minutes all had been said, and we were engaged to be married.

Our studios were opposite each other, separated by a wide hall, and it had been our custom, when one went to luncheon, for the other to sit with open door, so that visitors to the absent one might be seen and attended to. Emma generally lunched at a quiet restaurant near by, much frequented by ladies, and where an occasional male visitor might be seen, and to this place I also went as soon as she came back. I knew her favorite little table in the corner, and I always tried to occupy the place she had just vacated. But to-day we determined to lock our studio doors, and lunch together. There was really very little reason to expect a visitor. The waiter who attended to our wants was a quiet colored man, with white hair and whiskers, and an expression of kindly observation on his sable countenance. He arranged our table with much care, and listened to our orders with a deference I had not noticed before; but perhaps he always waited thus on ladies. While we were eating he retired to a little distance, and stood regarding us with an interested but not too intent attention. We had so often eaten at the same table, but never before at the same time.

When we returned we went first to my studio, and

when we opened the door the bull-calf seemed to smile. We both noticed it.

"There is something in the way he looks at us," said Emma, "that reminds me of our old waiter."

"Strange," I replied. "I noticed that myself."

Again I urged her to make the daisies for me, but she still refused.

"No," she said. "It is your picture, and you must not be unable to say that you did it all yourself. And, besides, if I were to put in any daisies, your calf is so natural that he would snip them off. I will not have my daisies snipped off, even by that handsome creature."

She looked up, as she said this, with a smile as bright and fresh as any daisy, and I— But never mind.

The next day we went again together to the restaurant, and the kindly observation deepened on the face of the waiter. When he had arranged with unusual nicety the little table service, he placed before Emma a wine-glass containing a button-hole bouquet. When we were leaving he detained me a moment, and said, in a low voice,

"After this, sir, if you would first order your beef for one with two plates, and then order the lady's chicken and salad for one with two plates, you would each have some beef and some chicken. It wouldn't cost any more, sir, and 'twould make more of a *menu*."

"'After this!'" I mentally repeated, as I gratefully put my hand in my pocket. If that old waiter had been an artist, what a gift his powers of observation would have been to him!

We agreed that we would be married in the early autumn, for truly there was little reason for delay. "It has been so many, many months," I said, "since I declared to myself that I would never marry any one but you that I really consider that I have been engaged to you for a very long time."

"I may as well admit that something of the same kind has passed through my mind. It is no harm to tell you so now, and it will make more of a *menu.*"

If my calf really cared to snip daisies, he must have envied me then.

There was no impediment to our early marriage except the fact that neither of us had any money.

"What you must do," said Emma, "is to finish your picture and sell it. You must stop looking at the calf you have at home. Of course he is growing every day, and new beauties are coming out on him all the time. You can not expect to have his picture keep pace with his development. After a while you will have to give him horns, and make him larger."

"The model is bigger now than the picture," I said; "and I must take your advice, and stop looking at him. If I don't, his portrait will never be done."

I would not put any flowers in the foreground, for, if I did so, I was sure they would look as if they had been picked out of a lady's bonnet. After what I had seen Emma do, I knew I could not paint daisies and buttercups. I put in some pale mullein leaves, and a point of rock which caught the light, and when this was done I determined to call the picture finished.

"What are you going to ask for it?" asked Emma.

"I had thought of a thousand dollars. Don't you consider that is a reasonable price?"

"I think it is a very low price," she answered, "considering the size of the picture and the admirable way in which it is painted. I imagine it is seldom that a picture like that is offered at a thousand dollars; but, as you want to sell it very much, I suppose it will be well not to ask any more."

"I do want very much to sell it," I said, giving her hand a squeeze which she understood.

I had also made up my mind in regard to the mode of disposing of the picture. Some weeks before, an artist friend in Boston had written to me that a well-known picture-dealer would open in that city early in September an art establishment particularly for the sale of pictures on commission, and that he would inaugurate his enterprise with an exhibition of paintings, which he wished to make as extensive and attractive as possible.

"If you have anything good, finished in time," wrote my friend, "I think you will do well to send it to Schemroth. He knows your work, and, if I mistake not, bought one of your pictures when he was in business in New York. I doubt if he has many animal subjects, and he wants variety. He says he is going to make his exhibition one of the art features of the season."

Emma agreed with me that I could not do better

than send my picture to Schemroth. He was an enterprising man, and would be certain to do everything he could to attract attention to his exhibition, and she felt sure that if the art public of Boston had a good opportunity of seeing my picture it would certainly be sold.

The painting was carefully packed, and sent to Boston, in care of my friend there, who shortly afterward wrote me that Schemroth liked it, and had given it a good place in his gallery, which would open in a day or two. My studio looked very bare and empty after the departure of my spirited bull-calf, so long my daily companion; but my mind was so occupied with the consideration of the important event which was to follow his sale that I did not miss him as much as I would otherwise have done. Emma and I talked a good deal about the best way of beginning our married life, and I was much in favor of a trip to Europe; but in regard to this she did not agree with me.

"A thousand dollars," she said, "would not go far for such a purpose. The steamer tickets would cost us about a hundred dollars apiece, and that would be four hundred dollars to go and come back. Then you certainly ought to keep a hundred dollars for your own use before you start, and that would only leave five hundred dollars with which to go to Paris and Rome and Dresden. If we did less than that, it would be hardly worth while to go at all. And five hundred dollars would not begin to be enough for two people."

I was obliged to admit that she was correct, and the European trip was given up.

"My idea is," said Emma, "that we ought to take

the money and furnish a house with it. That will be a good practical beginning, and after a while, when we have painted a few more pictures, we can go to Europe. You could keep a hundred dollars for your own use; we could put aside two hundred for rainy days or whatever kind of weather it may be when money is needed and there is none coming in, and then with seven hundred dollars we could buy enough furniture and other things to begin housekeeping in a small way. By this plan, you see, sir, your beautiful calf would give us an excellent start in life."

This proposition needed no discussion. Before she had half finished speaking I was convinced that nothing could be more sensible and delightful. "We must look for a house immediately," I said. "It won't do to put off that part of the business. We should know where we are going to live, so that when we are ready to buy the furniture there need be no delay."

Good fortunes as well as misfortunes sometimes object to coming singly; and just at this time I heard of something which was certainly a piece of rare good luck to a young couple contemplating matrimony. A gentleman named Osburn, who lived near my country home, with whom I had become well acquainted, and to whom I had confided the important news of my engagement, met me on the train a day or two after Emma and I had agreed upon the furniture project, and told me that if I intended to go to housekeeping he thought he could offer me a desirable opportunity. "My wife and I," he said, "wish very much to travel for a year or two, and the time has now arrived when we can do it, if we can dispose of our household effects, and get some one to take our house, on which we have a lease. Now if you are going to marry, and care for a place like ours, it might be worth your while to consider the question of taking it and buying our furniture. We will sell everything just as it is, excepting, of course, the books and such small articles as have a personal value, and you can walk right in and begin housekeeping at once. Everything was new two years ago, and you know my wife is a very careful housekeeper. The house is small and very simply furnished, and I have no doubt you would want to add all sorts of things, but at first you wouldn't really need anything that you wouldn't find there. We wish to dispose of the whole establishment — linen, china, silver (it's only plated, but it's very good), kitchen utensils, garden tools, a lot of fine poultry, a dog, a cat — everything, in fact, excepting the few articles I spoke of. What do you say?"

"Say!" I exclaimed; "there is nothing to say, except that I should be perfectly delighted to take the place off your hands if I could afford it; but I am afraid your price would be above my means. I suppose you would want to sell all or nothing?"

"Oh yes," said Mr. Osburn; "it would not pay us to sell out piecemeal, and we do not wish to let the house to any one who will not buy the furniture. If you think the proposition worth considering, my wife and I will make an estimate of what we consider the effects worth, and let you know."

I told him I should be very glad indeed to know,

and he said I should hear from him in a day or two.

When I told Emma of this, and described to her the Osburns' house, with its neat and comfortable furniture, its æsthetic wall-paper, its convenient and airy rooms, its well-kept garden and little lawn, its handsome barn and poultry-house, the wide pasture field belonging to it, the little patch of woodland at the upper end, the neatness and order of everything about the place; and all this at a very moderate rental, with a lease that had several years to run, she agreed with me that while it would be perfectly delightful to take this ready-made home off the Osburns' hands, there was no reason for us to hope that we should be able to do it. We should have to be content with something far less complete and perfect than this.

Two days after, I received a note from Osburn. "We have carefully considered the present value of our possessions," he said, "with an especial view of making it an object to you to buy them as a whole. Everything is in good order, but as we have had two years' use of the articles, we have considered that fact in making an estimate of what we think we ought to receive for them. After going over the matter several times we have determined to offer you the furniture and other things of which I spoke to you for seven hundred and fifty dollars."

"Why," cried Emma, as she read this letter over my shoulder (for I had taken it into her studio before I opened it), "that is only fifty dollars more than we had appropriated!"

"But we won't stop for that," I exclaimed.

"Stop!" she said, as with sparkling eyes and glowing cheeks she took both my hands in her own — regardless of the fact that she already held a brush heavily charged with Vandyck brown — "I should think not."

To work any more then was impossible for either of us. That afternoon we shut up both our studios, and went out to look at the paradise which had been offered us. Mr. Osburn had not yet come home, but his wife took great pleasure in making Emma's acquaintance and in showing us over the house and grounds. We found everything better of its kind, better adapted to the place in which it was, better suited to our every purpose, and altogether ever so much more desirable, than we had thought. I never saw Emma so enthusiastic. Even the picture of my bull-calf had not moved her thus. If the price had not been fixed beforehand, our delighted satisfaction would have been very impolitic. When Mr. Osburn returned I told him without hesitation that I would accept his offer. I think that he and his wife were almost as much pleased as we were. They had set their hearts on an extended tour in the South and far West. The lady's health demanded this, and her husband had found that he could now so arrange his business as to unite travel with profit; but it would have been impossible, as he afterward told me, for him to adopt this new mode of life without first disposing of his furniture and household goods. Ready money, I fancy, was not abundant with him.

When we took leave of the Osburns four people in

very high spirits stood shaking hands in the porch of the pretty house in which we had decided to make our home. There was an extraordinarily good point in this extraordinary piece of good fortune which had befallen us. If the Osburns had wished to settle the business with us at once it would, of course, have been impossible for us to do our part, but it would be at least six weeks before they intended to give up their house, and in that time we felt quite sure that my picture would be sold. But although we could take no actual steps toward making our arrangements for housekeeping, there was nothing to prevent our thinking and talking about them, and planning what was to be done; and this occupied a great deal of our time, much to the detriment, I am sure, of our daily work. We were always finding new good points in the matter.

"The only things about the Osburn house that I don't like," said Emma, "are the pictures and the bric-à-brac. Now these are the things that they want to keep, and if we are well off in any way, it is in pictures, and we can just take some of the paintings we have on hand, and a lot of our large engravings, and have them framed, and with that old armor and brass and china which you have collected, and which an animal painter doesn't want in his studio anyway, we can make our house look just lovely. I have collected too, and I have a good many nice things in my room which you have never seen."

"The house is a good one now," I exclaimed, "but it will look like another place when you and I get into it. And there is another thing that I have been thinking about. Of course I'll take my calf over there the first thing, and he will get a great deal better eating in that meadow than he has now. But he won't be the only animal we shall have. I intend to have a little model farm; that is to say, a farm on which we will keep models. Of course we shall have a cow, and she will not only give us milk and butter, but I can paint her. There is a fine little barn and stable on the place, but Osburn says he never thought he ought to keep a horse, because the house is only five minutes from the station, and it would be a piece of sheer extravagance for him to have a horse merely to drive about after he came home at night. But it wouldn't be extravagant in me; it would be actual economy. I ought to paint horses, and to do so properly and economically I should own one. And so with all sorts of animals. If I buy a fine dog or a beautiful cat, it will actually be money in my pocket."

"That is true," said Emma; "but you mustn't bring any wild animals there until they are so dead that you can wheel them home in a wheelbarrow. It will be perfectly delightful to have a horse, and, as I intend to paint birds as well as flowers, I can begin on the hens and little chickens and the ducks; and the sparrows and robins, if I can make them tame enough for me to sketch them."

"Yes," I exclaimed, "and you can paint the wild flowers in your own field; and we'll raise splendid Jacqueminot roses, and the hybrid tea, and other fine kinds; and we'll fix up a room for them in the winter, so that you can always have flowers for models at whatever stage you want them."

In the weeks that followed we paid several visits to the Osburns by their invitation, during which the husband explained to me the management of the celery beds, and many of his out-door improvements, while the wife had some long conversations with Emma about her household arrangements.

As the time approached when the Osburns wished to give up their house, Emma and I became very anxious to hear from Boston. I had written to my friend there explaining the situation, and he had promised to attend to the matter, and see that Schemroth communicated with me as soon as the picture was sold; so there was nothing to do but wait. I frequently met Mr. Osburn on the train, and I began to feel, as the time passed on, that I ought to be able to say something to him about concluding our bargain.

Of course he must have his preparations to make, and he would not wish to delay them too long. Although there was no real reason for it, as we assured ourselves over and over, both Emma and I began to be very uneasy, and we sometimes even regretted that we had accepted Mr. Osburn's offer. If we had not complicated the affair in this way we could have calmly waited until the picture was sold, and have then done what seemed to us best. There was no probability that we would have met with so good an opportunity of going to housekeeping, but we should have been independent and easy in our minds. But now we were neither. The plans and prospects of others depended upon us, and our uneasiness and anxiety increased every day. I disliked to meet Mr. Osburn, and every morning hoped that he would not be on the train. Never did I await the arrival of the mails with more anxiety and impatience.

One day, as Emma and I were returning from luncheon, the janitor of the building met us at the door. "A box came for you, sir, by express," he said. "I paid two dollars and twenty cents on it. It is up in your room."

I said nothing, but put my hand in my pocket. I began to count the money in my pocket-book, but my hand shook, and I dropped a quarter of a dollar on the floor, which rolled off to some distance. As the janitor went to pick it up, Emma approached me, and I noticed that she was very pale.

"If you haven't enough," she said, "I have some change with me."

I needed seventy cents to make up the sum, and Emma gave it to me. And then, without a word, we went upstairs. We did not hurry, but it was the first time, I think, that I ever became out of breath in going up those stairs. The moment we looked at the box we knew. The picture had been sent back.

I gazed at it blankly, reading over and over the painted address.

"Perhaps you had better open it," said Emma, in a very low voice. "It may not be—"

As quickly as I could I took off the center board. The bull-calf, with a melancholy greeting in his eyes, looked out upon us. Then Emma sat down upon the nearest chair and burst into tears, and I drew near to comfort her.

Half an hour later I had taken the picture from the box, which I carefully searched. "Do you know," I cried, a sudden anger taking the place of the deadened sensation of my heart, "that this is an outrageous insult? He should have written to me before he sent it back; but to return it, without a word or line of any kind, is simply brutal."

I said a great deal more than this. I was very angry. I would write to Schemroth, and let him know what I thought of this. Emma now endeavored to soothe my passion, and urged me not to do anything in a moment of excitement which might injure me in a business point of view. I did not promise forbearance, but suddenly exclaimed: "And then there is Osburn! He must be told. It will be a hard, hard thing to do! They will both be terribly disappointed. It will break up all their plans."

"I have thought about the Osburns," said Emma, coming close to me, and putting her hands upon my arm, "and I will tell you what we will do. I will go and see Mrs. Osburn. That will be much better than for you to see her husband. She will not be angry, and I can explain everything to her so that she will understand."

"No, my dear," said I; "that will not do. I shall not suffer you to bear what must be the very heaviest brunt of this trouble. In a case like this it is the duty of the man to put himself forward. I must go immediately and see Osburn at his office before he starts for home."

"I wish you would not," she said, earnestly. "Of course the man ought to take the lead in most things, but there may be times when it will be easier and better for the wife to go first."

The moment she said these words she blushed, and I snatched her into my arms. The wife! If those rich lovers of art had only known what they might have made of this dear girl by buying my picture, it would never have come back to me.

But time was flying, and if I was to see Osburn at his office, I must hurry. The thing was hard enough to do, as it was, and I did not feel that I could have the heart to tell the story in the presence of his wife.

"If he is very much troubled," said Emma, "and says anything to you which you do not like, you will not let him make you angry, will you?"

"Oh no," said I; "I am not so unreasonable as that. I have so much pity for him that he may say to me what he pleases. I will bear it all."

"I am very sorry for you," said Emma, looking up at me, "and I do wish you would let me see Mrs. Osburn."

But I was firm in my resolution not to shift this very unpleasant duty upon Emma, and in a few minutes I had started down-town. When I reached Mr. Osburn's place of business I found that he had gone home, although it was several hours earlier than his usual time of leaving. "He had something he wanted to attend to at his house," said one of the clerks.

This was a great disappointment to me, for now I would be obliged to go to see him that evening, and most probably to tell him the bad news in the presence of his wife. I did not fully appreciate until now how much easier it would have been to talk to him at his desk in the city. As I walked toward the Osburns' house just after dark that evening I could scarcely believe that I was going to the place which I had lately visited with such delight. Emma and I had fallen into the way of already considering the house and grounds as our own, and as I opened the gate I remembered how we had stood there while I told her about some improvements I intended to make in said gate, so that the weight and chain would never fail to latch it. And now it made no difference to me whether the gate latched or not. And the flower borders, too, on each side of the path! How Emma had talked to me, when we had walked far enough away, so as to be sure not to hurt Mrs. Osburn's feelings, of what she intended to do in those borders! It all seemed to me like visiting the grave of a home. But I walked steadily up to the house. The parlor shutters were wide open, and the room was brightly lighted, so that I could see plainly what was passing within. There was an air of disorder about the pretty room. Mr. Osburn, in his shirt sleeves, was on a step-ladder taking down a picture from the wall, while his wife stood below ready to receive it. All the other pictures—the portraits of their parents and the chromos which Emma and I thought so little of, but which they valued so highly—had been already taken down. These, with various little articles of ornament and use, valuable to them on account of association with some dear friend or some dear time, were the things which they intended to reserve; and it was plain that it was to take down and pack up these that Mr. Osburn had come home early that day. It was now only four days from the date he had fixed for surrendering the house to me, and he was working hard to have everything ready for us. He knew very well that Emma and I had arranged that we would be quietly married as soon as the house should be ours, and that in this charming home, all ready to our hands, we would immediately begin our married life. How earnestly and honestly they were doing their part!

I do not think I am a coward, but as I stood and gazed at these two I felt that it would be simply impossible for me to walk into that room and tell them that they might hang up their pictures again and unpack their bric-à-brac, and that they were not going to take the pleasant journeys they had planned, until they had found some other person, more able to keep to his word than I was, who should take their house and buy their goods.

No, I could not do it. I would go home and write to Osburn. I did not feel that this was as manly a course as to speak to him face to face, but I could not speak to him now. As I was about to turn away, Osburn got down from the ladder, and they both looked around the room. Their faces wore an expression of pleasant satisfaction at the conclusion of their task, but mingled, I truly believe, with a feeling of regret that they should leave to us such bare walls. How Emma and I had talked of what we intended to do with those walls! How I had drawn little sketches of them, and how we had planned and arranged for every space!

I hurried home, wrote a note, and tore it up. I wrote another, but that too did not properly express the situation. It was late, and I could do no more. I would write in the morning, take the letter into town and show it to Emma, and then send it to Osburn at the office.

The next day Emma was in my studio reading the disgraceful confession I had written, when the janitor came in, and handed me a letter.

"It is from Osburn," I exclaimed, glancing at the address, as the man closed the door behind him. "I know his handwriting. Now this is too bad. If Schemroth had only treated me with decent politeness I could have seen Osburn, or have written to him, before he felt himself obliged to remind me that the time had come for me to attend to my part of the contract."

"But you must not allow yourself to be so disturbed," said Emma. "You don't know what he has written."

"That is the only thing he could write about," said I, bitterly, as I opened the letter. "It is very humiliating."

We read the note together. It was very brief, and ran thus:

"DEAR SIR, — I have a customer who is willing to buy your picture, but he is dissatisfied with the foreground. If you will put in some daisies or other field flowers to brighten it up and throw the animal a little back, he will take it. I can ask him enough to cover your price and my commission. As I am sure you will make the alterations, I will forward the picture to you immediately.
"Yours truly,
L. SCHEMROTH."

The letter had been written four days previously.

We looked at each other, unable to speak. Our great cloud had turned completely over, and its lining dazzled us. We found words very soon, but I will not repeat them here. We could have fallen down and worshipped our painted calf.

"And now, my darling," I cried, "will you put the daisies in our picture?"

"Indeed will I," she said. And away she ran for her paints and brushes.

The rest of that afternoon she steadily painted, while I sat beside her, watching every touch of her brush.

"This daisy," she said, as she finished the first one, "is to make you happy, and the next one will be for myself; then I will paint two more for Mr. and Mrs. Osburn, and you must not fail to go and tell them to-night that you will settle up our business in a very short time; and I will paint a small daisy for Mr. Schemroth, and if he hadn't forgotten to mail his letter when it was written I would have made his daisy bigger."

The picture soon went back to Boston, and the original of it now spends most of his time looking over the fence of his pasture into the pretty yard of the house where the Osburns used to live, and hoping that some one will come and give him some cabbage leaves. If he could see all that there is to be seen he would see that the parlor of that house is hung with the spoils from the studios of two artists, that there is a room in the second story, with a northern light, in which flowers grow on canvas as beautifully as they grow in the fields and garden, and where a large picture is steadily progressing in which he figures as "The Coming Monarch." He would also see, far away on the Pacific shore, another couple whom he has helped to make happy; and if he could cast his eyes Bostonward he would see, every now and then, Mr. Schemroth writing to me to know when I could send him other animal pictures, and assuring me that he can find ready and profitable sale for all that I can paint. And, best of all, he could see, every day, Emma painting daisies into my life.

THE DISCOURAGER OF HESITANCY.

A CONTINUATION OF "THE LADY, OR THE TIGER?"

IT was nearly a year after the occurrence of that event in the arena of the semi-barbaric King known as the incident of the lady or the tiger, that there came to the palace of this monarch a deputation of five strangers from a far country. These men, of venerable and dignified aspect and demeanor, were received by a high officer of the court, and to him they made known their errand.

"Most noble officer," said the speaker of the deputation, "it so happened that one of our countrymen was present here, in your capital city, on that momentous occasion when a young man who had dared to aspire to the hand of your King's daughter had been placed in the arena, in the midst of the assembled multitude, and ordered to open one of two doors, not knowing whether a ferocious tiger would spring out upon him, or a beauteous lady would advance, ready to become his bride. Our fellow-citizen who was then present was a man of super-sensitive feelings, and at the moment when the youth was about to open the door he was so fearful lest he should behold a horrible spectacle, that his nerves failed him, and he fled precipitately from the arena, and mounting his camel rode homeward as fast as he could go.

"We were all very much interested in the story which our countryman told us, and we were extremely sorry that he did not wait to see the end of the affair. We hoped, however, that in a few weeks some traveler from your city would come among us and bring us further news; but up to the day when we left our country, no such traveler had arrived. At last it was determined that the only thing to be done was to send a deputation to this country, and to ask the question: 'Which came out of the open door, the lady, or the tiger?'"

When the high officer had heard the mission of this most respectable deputation, he led the five strangers into an inner room, where they were seated upon soft cushions, and where he ordered coffee, pipes, sherbet, and other semi-barbaric refreshments to be served to them. Then, taking his seat before them, he thus addressed the visitors:

"Most noble strangers, before answering the question you have come so far to ask, I will relate to you an incident which occurred not very long after that to which you have referred. It is well known in all regions hereabouts that our great King is very fond of the presence of beautiful women about his court. All the ladies-in-waiting upon the Queen and Royal Family are most lovely maidens, brought here from every part of the kingdom. The fame of this concourse of beauty, unequaled in any other royal court, has spread far and wide; and had it not been for the equally wide-spread fame of the systems of impetuous justice adopted by our King, many foreigners would doubtless have visited our court.

"But not very long ago there arrived here from a distant land a prince of distinguished appearance and undoubted rank. To such an one, of course, a royal audience was granted, and our King met him very graciously, and begged him to make known the object of his visit. Thereupon the Prince informed his Royal Highness that, having heard of the superior beauty of the ladies of his court, he had come to ask permission to make one of them his wife.

"When our King heard this bold announcement, his face reddened, he turned uneasily on his throne, and we were all in dread lest some quick words of furious condemnation should leap from out his quivering lips. But by a mighty effort he controlled himself; and after a moment's silence he turned to the Prince, and said: 'Your request is granted. To-morrow at noon you shall wed one of the fairest damsels of our court.' Then turning to his officers, he said: 'Give orders that everything be prepared for a wedding in this palace at high noon to-morrow. Convey this royal Prince to suitable apartments. Send to him tailors, boot-makers, hatters, jewelers, armorers; men of every craft, whose services he may need. Whatever he asks, provide. And let all be ready for the ceremony to-morrow.'

"'But, your Majesty,' exclaimed the Prince, 'before we make these preparations, I would like —— '

"'Say no more!' roared the King. 'My royal orders have been given, and nothing more is needed to be said. You asked a boon; I granted it; and I will hear no more on the subject. Farewell, my Prince, until to-morrow noon.'

"At this the King arose, and left the audience chamber, while the Prince was hurried away to the apartments selected for him. And here came to him tailors, hatters, jewelers, and every one who was needed to fit him out in grand attire for the wedding. But the mind of the Prince was much troubled and perplexed.

"'I do not understand,' he said to his attendants, 'this precipitancy of action. When am I to see the ladies, that I may choose among them? I wish opportunity, not only to gaze upon their forms and faces, but to become acquainted with their relative intellectual development.'

"'We can tell you nothing,' was the answer. 'What our King thinks right, that will he do. And more than this we know not.'

"'His Majesty's notions seem to be very peculiar,' said the Prince, 'and, so far as I can see, they do not at all agree with mine.'

"At that moment an attendant whom the Prince had not noticed before came and stood beside him. This was a broad-shouldered man of cheery aspect, who carried, its hilt in his right hand, and its broad back resting on his broad arm, an enormous scimeter, the upturned edge of which was keen and bright as any razor. Holding this formidable weapon as tenderly as though it had been a sleeping infant, this man drew closer to the Prince and bowed.

"'Who are you?' exclaimed his Highness, starting back at the sight of the frightful weapon.

"'I,' said the other, with a courteous smile, 'am the Discourager of Hesitancy. When our King makes known his wishes to any one, a subject or visitor, whose disposition in some little points may be supposed not to wholly coincide with that of his Majesty, I am appointed to attend him closely, that, should he think of pausing in the path of obedience to the royal will, he may look at me, and proceed.'

"The Prince looked at him, and proceeded to be measured for a coat.

"The tailors and shoemakers and hatters worked all night; and the next morning, when everything was ready, and the hour of noon was drawing nigh, the Prince again anxiously inquired of his attendants when he might expect to be introduced to the ladies.

"'The King will attend to that,' they said. 'We know nothing of the matter.'

"'Your Highness,' said the Discourager of Hesitancy, approaching with a courtly bow, 'will observe the excellent quality of this edge.' And drawing a hair from his head, he dropped it upon the upturned edge of his scimeter, upon which it was cut in two at the moment of touching.

"The Prince glanced and turned upon his heel.

"Now came officers to conduct him to the grand hall of the palace, in which the ceremony was to be performed. Here the Prince found the King seated on the throne, with his nobles, his courtiers, and his officers standing about him in magnificent array. The Prince was led to a position in front of the King, to whom he made obeisance, and then said:

"'Your Majesty, before I proceed further——'

"At this moment an attendant, who had approached with a long scarf of delicate silk, wound it about the lower part of the Prince's face so quickly and adroitly that he was obliged to cease speaking. Then, with wonderful dexterity, the rest of the scarf was wound around the Prince's head, so that he was completely blindfolded. Thereupon the attendant quickly made openings in the scarf over the mouth and ears, so that the Prince might breathe and hear; and fastening the ends of the scarf securely, he retired.

"The first impulse of the Prince was to snatch the silken folds from his head and face; but as he raised his hands to do so, he heard beside him the voice of the Discourager of Hesitancy, who gently whispered: 'I am here, your Highness.' And, with a shudder, the arms of the Prince fell down by his side.

"Now before him he heard the voice of a priest, who had begun the marriage service in use in that semi-barbaric country. At his side he could hear a delicate rustle, which seemed to proceed from fabrics of soft silk. Gently putting forth his hand, he felt folds of such silk close beside him. Then came the voice of the priest requesting him to take the hand of the lady by his side; and reaching forth his right hand, the Prince received within it another hand so small, so soft, so delicately fashioned, and so delightful to the touch, that a thrill went through his being. Then, as was the custom of the country, the priest first asked the lady would she have this man to be her husband. To which the answer gently came in the sweetest voice he ever heard: 'I will.'

"Then ran raptures rampant through the Prince's blood. The touch, the tone, enchanted him. All the ladies of that court were beautiful; the Discourager was behind him; and through his parted scarf he boldly answered: 'Yes, I will.'

"Whereupon the priest pronounced them man and wife.

"Now the Prince heard a little bustle about him; the long scarf was rapidly unrolled from his head; and he turned, with a start, to gaze upon his bride. To his utter amazement, there was no one there. He stood alone. Unable on the instant to ask a question or say a word, he gazed blankly about him.

"Then the King arose from his throne, and came down, and took him by the hand.

"'Where is my wife?' gasped the Prince.

"'She is here,' said the King, leading him to a curtained doorway at the side of the hall.

"The curtains were drawn aside, and the Prince, entering, found himself in a long apartment, near the opposite wall of which stood a line of forty ladies, all dressed in rich attire, and each one apparently more beautiful than the rest.

"Waving his hand towards the line, the King said to the Prince: 'There is your bride! Approach, and lead her forth! But remember this: that if you attempt to take away one of the unmarried damsels of our court, your execution shall be instantaneous. Now, delay no longer. Step up and take your bride.'

"The Prince, as in a dream, walked slowly along the line of ladies, and then walked slowly back again. Nothing could he see about any one of them to indicate that she was more of a bride than the others. Their dresses were all similar; they all blushed; they all looked up, and then looked down. They all had charming little hands. Not one spoke a word. Not one lifted a finger to make a sign. It was evident that the orders given them had been very strict.

"'Why this delay?' roared the King. 'If I had been married this day to one so fair as the lady who wedded you, I should not wait one second to claim her.'

"The bewildered Prince walked again up and down the line. And this time there was a slight change in the countenances of two of the ladies. One of the fairest gently smiled as he passed her. Another, just as beautiful, slightly frowned.

"'Now,' said the Prince to himself, 'I am sure that it is one of those two ladies whom I have married. But which? One smiled. And would not any woman smile when she saw, in such a case, her husband coming towards her? But, then, were she not his bride, would she not smile with satisfaction to think he had not selected her, and that she had not led him to an untimely doom? Then again, on the other hand, would not any woman frown when she saw her husband come towards her and fail to claim her? Would she not knit her lovely brows? And would she not inwardly say, "It is I! Don't you know it? Don't you feel it? Come!" But if this woman had not been married, would she not frown when she saw the man looking at her? Would she not say to herself, "Don't stop at me! It is the next but one. It is two ladies above. Go on!" And then again, the one who married me did not see my face. Would she not smile if she thought me comely? While if I wedded the one who frowned, could she restrain her disapprobation if she did not like me? Smiles invite the approach of true love. A frown is a reproach to a tardy advance. A smile ——'

"'Now, hear me!' loudly cried the King. 'In ten seconds, if you do not take the lady we have given you, she, who has just been made your bride, shall be your widow.'

"And, as the last word was uttered, the Discourager of Hesitancy stepped close behind the Prince, and whispered: 'I am here!'

"Now the prince could not hesitate an instant; and he stepped forward and took one of the two ladies by the hand.

"Loud rang the bells; loud cheered the people; and the King came forward to congratulate the Prince. He had taken his lawful bride.

"Now, then," said the high officer to the deputation of five strangers from a far country, "When you can decide among yourselves which lady the Prince chose, the one who smiled or the one who frowned, then will

I tell you which came out of the opened door, the lady or the tiger!"

At the latest accounts the five strangers had not yet decided.

A BORROWED MONTH.

EAST.

ALL persons who, like myself, are artists, and all others who delight in the beauties of lake and valley, the grandeur of snowy mountain peaks, and the invigoration of pure mountain air, can imagine the joy with which I found myself in Switzerland on a sketching tour. It had not been easy for me to make this, my first visit to Europe. Circumstances, which the very slightly opened purses of my patrons had not enabled me to control, had deferred it for several years. And even now my stay was strictly limited, and I must return by a steamer which sailed for America early in the autumn. But I had already traveled a good deal on the Continent; had seen Italy; and now had six summer weeks to give to Switzerland. Six months would have suited me much better, but youth and enthusiasm can do a great deal of sketching and nature-reveling in six weeks.

I began what I called my Alpine holidays in a little town not far from the upper end of Lake Geneva, and at the close of my second day of rambling and sketching I was attacked by a very disagreeable and annoying pain in my left leg. It did not result, so far as I could ascertain, from a sprain, a bruise, or a break, but seemed to be occasioned by a sort of tantalizing rheumatism; for while it entirely disappeared when I remained at rest, its twinges began as soon as I had taken half-a-dozen steps in walking. The next day I consulted a doctor, and he gave me a lotion. This, however, was of no service, and for three or four days he made use of other remedies, none of which were of the slightest benefit to me.

But, although I was confined to the house during this period, I did not lose my time. From the windows of my room in the hotel I had a series of the most enchanting views, which I sketched from early morning until twilight, with an earnest and almost ecstatic zeal. On the other side of the lake rose, ten thousand feet in the air, the great Dent du Midi, with its seven peaks clear and sharp against the sky, surrounded by its sister mountains, most of them dark of base and white of tip. To the east stretched the beautiful valley of the Rhone, up which the view extended to the pale-blue pyramid of Mont Vélan. Curving northward around the end of the lake was a range of lower mountains, rocky or verdant; while at their base, glistening in the sun, lay the blue lake reflecting the white clouds in the sky, and dotted here and there with little vessels, their lateen-sails spread out like the wings of a descending bird.

I sketched and painted the lake and mountains, by the light of morning, in their noontide splendors, and when all lay in shadow except where the highest snowy peaks were tipped with the rosy afterglow. My ailment gave me no trouble at all so long as I sat still and painted, and in the wonderful opportunity afforded by nature to my art I forgot all about it.

But in the course of a week I began to get very impatient. There was a vast deal more of Switzerland to be seen and sketched; my time was growing short, and the pain occasioned by walking had not abated in the least. I felt that I must have other views than those which were visible from my window, and I had myself driven to various points accessible to vehicles, from which I made some very satisfactory sketches. But this was not roaming in Alpine valleys and climbing mountain peaks. It was only a small part of what brought me to Switzerland, and my soul rebelled. Could any worse fate befall a poor young artist, who had struggled so hard to get over here, than to be thus chained and trammeled in the midst of the grandest opportunities his art life had yet known?

My physician gave me but little comfort. He assured me that if I used his remedies and had patience, there would be no doubt of my recovery; but that it would take time. When I eagerly asked how much time would be required, he replied that it would probably be some weeks before I was entirely well, for these disorders generally wore off quite gradually.

"Some weeks!" I ejaculated when he had gone. "And I have barely a month left for Switzerland!"

This state of affairs not only depressed me, but it disheartened me. I might have gone by rail to other parts of Switzerland, and made other sketches from hotels and carriages, but this I did not care to do. If I must still carry about with me my figurative ball and chain, I did not wish to go where new temptations would beckon and call and scream to me from every side. Better to remain where I was; where I could more easily become used to my galling restraints. This was morbid reasoning, but I had become morbid in body and mind.

One evening I went in the hotel omnibus to the Kursaal of the little town where I was staying. In this building, to which visitors from the hotels and *pensions* of the vicinity went in considerable numbers every afternoon and evening, for the reason that they had nothing else to do, the usual concert was going on in the theater. In a small room adjoining, a company of gentlemen and ladies, the latter chiefly English or Russian, were making bets on small metal horses and jockeys which spun round on circular tracks, and ran races which were fairer to the betters than the majority of those in which flesh-and-blood animals, human and equine, take part. Opening from this apartment was a large refreshment-room, in which I took my seat. Here I could smoke a cigar and listen to the music, and perhaps forget for a time the doleful world in which I lived. I had not been long seated before I was joined by a man whom I had met before, and in whom I had taken some interest. He was a little man with a big head, on which he occasionally wore a high-crowned black straw hat; but whenever the sun did not make it absolutely necessary he carried this in his hand. His clothes were black and of very thin material, and he always had the appearance of being too warm. In my occasional interviews with him I had discovered that he was a reformer, and that his yearnings in the direction of human improvement were very general and inclusive.

This individual sat down at my little table and ordered a glass of beer.

"You do not look happy," he said. "Have you spoiled a picture?"

"No," I replied, "but a picture has been spoiled for me." And, as he did not understand this reply, I explained to him how the artistic paradise which I had mentally painted for myself had been scraped from the canvas by the knife of my malicious ailment.

"I have been noticing," he said, — he spoke very fair English, but it was not his native tongue, — "that you have not walked. It is a grand pity." And he stroked his beard and looked at me steadfastly. "An artist who is young is free," he said, after some moments' reflection. "He is not obliged to carry the load of a method which has grown upon him like the goître of one of these people whom you meet here. He can despise methods and be himself. You have everything in art before you, and it is not right that you should be held to the ground like a serpent in your own country, with a forked stick. You have some friends, perhaps?"

I replied, a little surprised, that I had a great many friends in America.

"It is of no import where they are," he said. And then he again regarded me in silence. "Have you a good faith?" he presently asked.

"In what?" said I.

"In anything. Yourself, principally."

I replied that just now I had very little faith of that sort.

His face clouded; he frowned, and, pushing away his empty glass, he rose from the table. "You are a skeptic," he said, "and an infidel of the worst sort."

In my apathetic state this remark did not annoy me. "No man would be a skeptic," I said carelessly, "if other people did not persist in disagreeing with him."

But my companion paid no attention to me, and walked away before I had finished speaking. In a few minutes he came back, and, leaning over the table, he said in low but excited tones: "It is to yourself that you are an infidel. That is very wrong. It is degrading."

"I do not understand you at all," I said. "Won't you sit down and tell me what you mean?"

He seated himself, and wiped his forehead with his handkerchief. Then he fixed his eyes upon me, and said: "It is not to everybody I would speak as I now speak to you. You must believe something. Do you not believe in the outstretching power of the mind; of the soul?"

My ideas in this regard were somewhat chaotic. I did not know what was his exact meaning, but I thought it best to say that it was likely that some souls could outstretch.

"And do you not believe," he continued, "that when your friend sleeps, and your thoughts are fixed upon him, and your whole soul goes out to him in its most utter force and strength, that your mind becomes his mind?"

I shook my head. "That is going rather far," I said.

"It is not far," he exclaimed emphatically. "It is but a little way. We shall go much farther than that when we know more. And is it that you doubt that the mind is in the brain? And where is pain? Is it in the foot? In the arm? It is not so. It is in the brain. If you cut off your wounded foot, you have the pain all the same; the brain remains. I will say this to you. If it were I who had soul-friends, it would not be that every day I should shut the door on my art. Once it happened that I suffered — not like you, much worse. But I did not suffer every day. No, no, my friend, not every day. But that was I; I have faith. But I need speak no more to you. You are infidel. You do not believe in yourself."

And with this he suddenly pushed back his chair, picked up his black straw hat from the floor, and walked out of the room, wiping his forehead as he went. I am not given to sudden reciprocations of sentiment, but what this man had said made a strong impression upon me. Not that I had any confidence in the value of his psychological ideas, but his words suggested a train of thought which kept me awake a long time after I had gone to bed that night; and gradually I began to consider the wonderful advantage and help it would be to me if it were possible that a friend could bear my infirmity even for a day. It would inconvenience him but little. If he remained at rest he would feel no pain, and he might be very glad to be obliged to take a quiet holiday with his books or family. And what a joy would that holiday be to me among the Alps, and relieved of my fetters! The notion grew. One day one friend might take up my burden, and the next another. How little this would be for them; how much for me! If I should select thirty friends, they could, by each taking a day of pleasant rest, make me free to enjoy to the utmost the month which yet remained for Switzerland. My mind continued to dwell on this pleasing fancy, and I went to sleep while counting on my fingers the number of friends I had who would each be perfectly willing to bear for a day the infirmity which was so disastrous to me, but which would be of such trifling importance to them.

I woke very early in the morning, and my thoughts immediately recurred to the subject of my ailment and my friends. What a pity it was that such an advantageous arrangement should be merely whim and fancy! But if my companion of the night before were here, he would tell me that there was no impossibility, only a want of faith — faith in the power of mind over mind, of mind over body, and, primarily, of faith in my own mind and will. I smiled as I thought of what might happen if his ideas were based on truth. There was my friend Will Troy. How gladly would he spend a day at home in his easy-chair, smoking his pipe and forgetting, over a novel, that there were such things as ledgers, day-books, and columns of figures, while I strode gayly over the mountain sides. If Troy had any option in the matter, he would not hesitate for a moment;

and, knowing this, I would not hesitate for a moment in making the little arrangement, if it could be made. If belief in myself could do it, it would be done; and I began to wonder if it were possible, in any case, for a man to believe in himself to such an extent.

Suddenly I determined to try. "It is early morning here," I said to myself, "and in America it must be about the middle of the night, and Will Troy is probably sound asleep. Let me then determine, with all the energy of my mental powers, that my mind shall be his mind, and that he shall understand thoroughly that he has some sort of trouble in his left leg which will not inconvenience him at all if he allows it to rest, but which will hurt him very much if he attempts to walk about. Then I will make up my mind, quite decidedly, that for a day it shall be Will who will be subject to this pain, and not I."

For half an hour I lay flat on my back, my lips firmly pressed together, my hands clinched, and my eyes fixed upon the immutable peaks of the Dent du Midi, which were clearly visible through the window at the foot of my bed. My position seemed to be the natural one for a man bending all the energies of his mind on a determinate purpose. The great mountain stood up before me as an example of the steadfast and immovable. "Now," said I to myself, over and over again, "Will Troy, it is you who are subject to this trouble. You will know exactly what it is, because you will feel it through my mind. I am free from it; I will that, and it shall be so. My mind has power over your mind, because yours is asleep and passive, while mine is awake and very, very active. When I get out of bed I shall be as entirely free from pain and difficulty in walking as you would have been if I had not passed my condition over to you for one short day." And I repeated again and again: "For one day; only for one day."

The most difficult part of the process was the mental operation of believing all this. If I did not believe it, of course, it would come to nothing. Fixing my mind steadfastly upon this subject, I believed with all my might. When I had believed for ten or fifteen minutes, I felt sure that my faith in the power of my mind was well grounded and fixed. A man who has truly believed for a quarter of an hour may be considered to have embraced a faith.

And now came the supreme moment, and when I arose should I be perfectly well and strong? The instant this question came into my mind I dismissed it. I would have no doubt whatever on the subject. I would *know* that I should be what I willed I should be. With my mind and my teeth firmly set, I got out of bed, I walked boldly to the window, I moved about the room, I dressed myself. I made no experiments; I would scorn to do so. Experiments imply doubt. I believed. I went down several flights of stairs to my breakfast. I walked the whole length of the long *salle-à-manger*, and sat down at the table without having felt a twinge of pain or the least discomfort.

"Monsieur is better this morning," said the head-waiter, with a kindly smile.

"Better," said I; "I am well."

When I returned that evening after a day of intoxicating delight, during which I had climbed many a mountain path, had stood on bluffs and peaks, had gazed over lake and valley, and had breathed to the full the invigorating upper air, I stood upon the edge of the lake, just before reaching the hotel, and stretched forth my hands to the west.

"I thank you, Will Troy," I said, "from the bottom of my heart I thank you for this day; and if I ever see my way to repay you, I will do it, my boy. You may be sure of that."

I now resolved to quit this place instantly. I had been here too long; and before me was spread out in shadowy fascination the whole of Switzerland. I took a night-train for Berne, where I arrived early the next day. But before I descended from the railway carriage, where I had managed to slumber for part of the night, I had determinately willed an interchange of physical condition with another friend in America. During the previous day I had fully made up my mind that I should be false to myself and to my fortunes if I gave up this grand opportunity for study and artistic development, and I would call upon my friends to give me these precious holidays, of which, but a little while ago, I believed myself forever deprived. I belonged to a club of artists, most of whom were young and vigorous fellows, any one of whom would be glad to do me a service; and although I desired on special occasions to interchange with particular friends, I determined that during the rest of my holiday I would, for the most part, exchange physical conditions with these young men, giving a day to each.

The next week was a perfect success. As Martyn, Jeffries, Williams, Corbell, Field, Booker, and Graham, I walked, climbed, sketched, and, when nobody was near, shouted with delight. I took Williams for Sunday, because I knew he never sketched on that day, although he was not averse to the longest kind of rural ramble. I shall not detail my route. The Bernese Oberland, the region of Lake Lucerne, the Engadine, and other earthly heavens opened their doors to my joyous anticipations, provided always that this system of physical exchange continued to work.

The Monday after Williams's Sunday I appropriated to a long tramp which should begin with a view of the sunrise from a mountain height, and which necessitated my starting in the morning before daylight. For such an excursion I needed all the strength and endurance of which I could possess myself, and I did not hesitate as to the exchange I should make for that long day's work. Chester Parkman was the man for me. Parkman was a fairly good artist, but the sphere in which he shone was that of the athlete. He was not very tall, but he was broad and well made, with a chest and muscles which to some of his friends appeared to be in an impertinent condition of perfect development. He was a handsome fellow, too, with his well-browned face, his fine white teeth, and his black hair and beard, which seemed to curl because the strength which they imbibed from him made it necessary to do something, and curling is all that hair can do. On some occasions it pleased me to think that when by the power of my will my physical incapacity was transferred for a time to a friend, I, in turn, found myself in his peculiar bodily condition, whatever it might be. And whether I was mistaken or not, and whether this phase of my borrowed condition was real or imaginary, it is certain that when I started out before dawn that Monday morning I strode away with vigorous Parkmanic legs, and inhaled the cool air into what seemed to be a deep Parkmanic chest. I took a guide that day, and when we returned, some time after nightfall, I could see that he was tired, and he admitted the fact; but as for me, I ate a good supper, and then walked a mile and a half to sketch a moonlight effect on a lake. I will here remark that, out of justice to Parkman, I rubbed myself down and polished myself off to the best of my knowledge and ability before I went to bed.

When, as usual, I awoke early the next morning, I lay for some time thinking. It had been my intention to spend that day in a boat on the lake, and I had decided to direct my will-power upon Tom Latham, a young collegian of my acquaintance. Tom was an enthusiastic oarsman, and could pull with such strength that if he were driving a horse he could almost haul the animal back into the vehicle, but if a stout boy were to be pushed off a horse-block Tom could not do it. Tom's unequally developed muscles were just what I wanted that day; but before I threw out my mind in his direction I let it dwell in pleasant recollection upon the glorious day I had had with Chester Parkman's corporeal attributes. Thinking of Chester, I began to think of some one else — one on whom my thoughts had rested with more pleasure and more pain than on any other person in the world. That this was a woman I need not say. She was young, she was an artist, and a very good friend of mine. For a long time I had yearned with all my heart to be able to say that she was more than this. But so far I could not say it. Since I had been in Europe I had told myself over and over that in coming away without telling Kate Balthis that I loved her I made the greatest mistake of my life. I had intended to do this, but opportunity had not offered. I should have made opportunity.

The reason that the thought of Chester Parkman made me think of Kate was the fact that they occupied studios in the same building, and that he was a great admirer not only of her work, but of herself. If it had not been for the existence of Parkman, I should not have blamed myself quite so much for not proposing to Kate before I left America. But I consoled myself by reflecting that the man was so intent upon the development of his lungs that his heart, to put it anatomically, was obliged to take a minor place in his consideration.

Thinking thus, a queer notion came into my head. Suppose that Kate were to bear my troubles for a day! What friend had I who would be more willing to serve me than she? And what friend from whom I would be more delighted to receive a favor? But the next instant the contemptibleness of this idea flashed across my mind, and I gritted my teeth as I thought what a despicable thing it would be to deprive that dear girl of her strength and activity, even for a day. It was true, as I honestly told myself, that it was the joy and charm of being beholden to her, and not the benefit to myself, that made me think of this thing. But it was despicable, all the same, and I utterly scouted it. And so, forgetting as far as possible that there was such a person in the world as Kate, I threw out my mind, as I originally intended, towards Tom Latham, the oarsman.

I spent that day on the lake. If I had been able to imagine that I could walk as far as Chester Parkman, I failed to bring myself to believe that I could row like young Latham. I got on well enough, but rowed no better than I had often done at home, and I was soon sorry that I had not brought a man with me to take the oars, of which I had tired.

Among those I called upon in the next few days was Professor Dynard, a man who was not exactly a friend, but with whom I was very well acquainted. He was a scientific man, a writer of books, and an enthusiastic lover of nature. He was middle-aged and stooped a little, but his legs were long, and he was an unwearied walker. Towards the end of the very pleasant day which I owed to my acquaintance with him, I could not help smiling to find that I had thought so much of the professor during my rambles that I had unconsciously adopted the stoop of his shoulder and his ungainly but regular stride.

The half-starved man to whom food is given eats too much; the child, released from long hours of school, runs wild, and is apt to make himself objectionable; and I, rising from my condition of what I had considered hopeless inactivity to the fullest vigor of body and limb, began to perceive that I had walked too much and worked too little. The pleasure of being able to ramble and scramble wherever I pleased had made me forget that I was in Switzerland not only for enjoyment, but for improvement. Of course I had to walk and climb to find points of view, but the pleasure of getting to such places was so great that it overshadowed my interest in sitting down and going to work after I had reached them. The man who sketches as he walks and climbs is an extraordinary artist, and I was not such a one.

It was while I was in the picturesque regions of the Engadine that these reflections forced themselves upon me, and I determined to live less for mere enjoyment and more for earnest work. But not for a minute did I think of giving up my precious system of corporeal exchange. I had had enough of sitting in my room and sketching from the window. If I had consented to allow myself to relapse into my former condition, I feared that I should not be able to regain that firm belief in the power of my mental propulsion which had so far enabled my friends to serve me so well, with such brief inconvenience to themselves. No. I would continue to transfer my physical incapacity, but I would use more conscientiously and earnestly the opportunities which I thus obtained.

Soon after I came to this determination, I established myself at a little hotel on a mountain-side, where I decided to stay for a week or more and do some good hard work; I was surrounded by grand and beautiful scenery, and it was far better for my progress in art to stay here and do something substantial than to wander about in search of fresh delights. As an appropriate beginning to this industrious period, I made an exchange with my friend Bufford, one of the hardest-working painters I knew. His industry as well as his genius had brought him, when he had barely reached middle life, to a high position in art, and it pleased me to think that I might find myself influenced by some of his mental characteristics as well as those of a physical nature. At any rate, I tried hard to think so, and I am not sure that I did not paint better on the Bufford day than on any other. If it had not been that I had positively determined that I would not impose my ailment upon any one of my friends for more than one day, I would have taken Bufford for a week.

There were a good many people staying at the hotel, and among them was a very pretty English girl, with whom I soon became acquainted; for she was an enthusiastic amateur artist, and was engaged in painting the same view at which I had chosen to work. Every morning she used to go some distance up the mountain-side, accompanied by her brother Dick, a tall, gawky boy of about eighteen, who was considered to be a suitable and sufficient escort, but who was in reality a very poor one, for no sooner was his sister comfortably seated at her work than he left her and rambled away for hours. If it had not been for me I think she would sometimes have been entirely too lonely and unprotected. Dick's appetite would generally bring him back in time to carry down her camp-chair and color-box when we returned to dinner; and as she never complained of his defections, I suppose her mother knew nothing about them. This lady was a very pleasant person, a little too heavy in body and a little too large in cap for my taste, but hearty and genial, and very anxious to know something about America, where her oldest son was established on a Texas ranch. She and her daughter and myself used to talk a good deal together in the evenings, and this intimacy made me feel quite justified in talking a good deal to the daughter in the mornings as we were working together on the mountain-side. The first thing that made me take an interest in this girl was the fact that she considered me her superior, and looked up to me. I could paint a great deal better than she could, and could inform her on a lot of points, and I was always glad to render her such service. She was a very pretty girl, — the prettiest English girl I ever saw, — with large, gray-blue eyes, which had a trustfulness about them which I liked very much. She evidently had a very good opinion of me as an artist, and paid as much earnest and thoughtful attention to what I said about her work as if she had really been the scholar and I the master. I tried not to bore her by too much technical conversation, and endeavored to make myself as agreeable a companion as I could. I found that fellowship of some kind was very necessary to a man so far away from home, and so cut off from social influences.

Day after day we spent our mornings together, sketching and talking; and as for Dick, he was the most interesting brother I ever knew. He had a great desire to discover something hitherto unknown in the heights above our place of sketching. Finding that he could depend on me as a protector for his sister, he gave us very little of his company. Even when we were not together I could not help thinking a great deal about this charming girl. Our talks about her country had made me remember with pride the English blood that was in me, and revived the desire I had often felt to live for a time, at least, in rural England, that land of loveliness to the Anglo-Saxon mind. And London too! I had artist friends, Americans, who lived in London, and such were their opportunities, such the art atmosphere and society, that they expected to live there always. If a fellow really wished to succeed as an artist, some years' residence in England, with an occasional trip to the Continent, would be a great thing for him. And, in such a case — well, it was a mere idle thought. If I had been an engaged man, I would not have allowed myself even such idle thoughts. But I was not engaged; and alas! I thought with a sigh, I might never be. I thought of Parkman and of Kate, and how they must constantly see each other; and I remembered my stupid silence when leaving America. How could I tell what had happened since my departure? I did not like to think of all this, and tried to feel resigned. The world was very wide. There was that English brother, over on the Texas ranch; he might marry an American girl; and here was his sister — well, this was all the merest nonsense, and I would not admit to myself that I attached the slightest importance to these vague and fragmentary notions which floated through my mind. But the girl had most lovely, trustful eyes, and I felt that a sympathy had grown up between us which must not be rudely jarred.

We had finished our work at the old sketching-place, and we proposed on the morrow to go to a higher part of the mountain, and make some sketches of a more extended nature than we had yet tried. This excursion would require a good part of the day, but we would take along a luncheon for three, and no doubt nothing would please Dick better than such a trip. The mother agreed, if Dick could be made to promise that he would take his sister by the hand when he came to any steep places. But, alas! when that youngster was called upon to receive his injunctions, he declared he could not accompany us. He had promised, he said, to go on a tramp with some of the other men, which would take him all day. And that, of course, put an end to our expedition. I shall not soon forget the air, charming to me, of evident sorrow and disappointment with which Beatrice told me this early in the evening. The next day was the only one for which such a trip could be planned, for, on the day following, two older sisters were expected, and then everything would be different. I, too, was very much grieved and disappointed, for I had expected a day of rare pleasure; but my regret was tempered by an intense satisfaction at perceiving how sorry she was. The few words she said on the subject touched me very much. She was such a true, honest-hearted girl that she could not conceal what she felt; and when we shook hands in bidding each other good-night, it was with more warmth than either of us had yet shown at the recurrence of this little ceremony.

When I went to my room I said to myself: "If she had not been prevented from going, I should never have known how glad she would be to go." The thought pleased me greatly, but I had no time to dwell upon it, for in came Dick, who, with his hands in his pockets and his legs very wide apart, declared to me that he had found his sister was so cut up by not being able to make those sketches on the mountain the next day, that he had determined to go with us.

"It will be a beastly shame to disappoint her," he said; "so you can get your traps together, and we will have an early breakfast and start off."

"Now," said I, when he had shut the door behind him, "I know how much she wanted to go, and she is going! Could anything be better than this?"

In making the physical transfers which were necessary at this period for my enjoyment of an outdoor excursion, I did not always bring my mental force to work upon an exchange of condition. Very often I was willing to send out my ailment to another, and to content myself with being for the day what I would be in my ordinary health. But in particular instances, such as those of Parkman and Bufford, I willed — and persuaded myself that I had succeeded — that certain desirable attributes of my benefactor for the day, which would be useless to him during his period of enforced restfulness, should be attracted to myself. Before I went to sleep I determined that on the following day I would exchange with my brother Philip, and would make it as absolute an exchange as my will could bring about. Phil was not an athlete, like Parkman, but he was a strong and vigorous fellow, with an immense deal of go in him. He was thoroughly good-natured, and I knew that he would be perfectly willing, if he could know all about it, to take a day's rest, and give me a day with Beatrice. And what a charming day that was to be! We did not know exactly where we were going, and we should have to explore. There would be steep places to climb, and it would not be Dick who would help his sister. We should have to rest, and we would rest together. There would be a delightful lunch under the shade of some rock. There would be long talks, and a charming coöperation in the selection of points of view and in work. Indeed, there was no knowing what might not come out of a day like that.

In the morning I made the transfer, and soon afterwards I arose. Before I was ready to go down-stairs I was surprised by an attack of headache, a thing very unusual with me. The pain increased so much that I was obliged to go back to bed. I soon found that I must give up the intended excursion, and I remained in bed all day. In the course of the afternoon, while I lay bemoaning my present misery as well as the loss of the great pleasure I had expected, a thought suddenly came into my mind, which, in spite of my miseries, made me burst out laughing. I remembered that my brother Phil, although enjoying, as a rule, the most vigorous good health, was subject to occasional attacks of sick headache, which usually laid him up for a day or two. Evidently I had struck him on one of his headache days. How relieved the old fellow must be to find his positive woe changed to a negative evil! It was very funny!

In the evening came Dick with a message from his mother and his sister Beatrice, who wanted to know how I felt by this time, and if I would have a cup of tea, or anything. "It's a beastly shame," said he, "that you got yourself knocked up in this way."

"Yes," said I, "but my misfortune is your good fortune, for, of course, you had your tramp with your friends."

"Oh, I should have had that any way," replied the good youth, "for I only intended to walk a mile or two up the mountain, just to satisfy the old lady, and then, without saying whether I was coming back or not, I intended to slip off and join the other fellows. Wouldn't that have been a jolly plan? Beatrice would have had her day, and I should have had mine. But *you* must go and upset her part of it."

When Dick had gone I reflected. What a day this would have been! Alone so long with Beatrice among those grand old mountains! As I continued to think of this I began to tremble, and the more I thought the more I trembled; and the reason I trembled was the conviction that if I had spent that day with her, I certainly should have proposed to her.

"Phil," I said, "I thank you. I thank you more for your headache than for anything else any other fellow could give me."

A sick headache, aided by conscience, can work a great change in a man. My soul condemned me for having come so near being a very false lover, and my mind congratulated me upon having the miss made for me, for I never should have been strong enough to make it for myself.

The next day the sisters arrived, and I saw but little of Beatrice, for which, although quite sorry, I was also very glad; and after a day on the mountain which I owed to Horace Bartlett, the last man in our club on whom I felt I could draw, I returned to the hotel, and wrote a long letter to Kate. I had informed my friends in America of the ailment which had so frustrated all my plans of work and enjoyment, but I had never written anything in regard to my novel scheme of relief. This was something which could be better explained by word of mouth when I returned. And, besides, I did not wish to say anything about it until the month of proposed physical transfers had expired. I wrote to Kate, however, that I was now able to walk and climb as much as I pleased, and in my repentant exuberance I hinted at a great many points which, although I knew she could not understand them, would excite her curiosity and interest in the remarkable story I would tell her when I returned. I tried to intimate, in the most guarded way, much that I intended to say to her when I saw her concerning my series of deliverances; and my satisfaction at having escaped a great temptation gave a kindly earnestness to my manner of expressing myself, which otherwise it might not have had.

There were now six days of my Swiss holiday left; and during these I threw myself upon the involuntary kindness of Mr. Henry Brinton, editor of a periodical entitled "Our Mother Earth," and upon that of his five assistants in the publishing and editorial departments. Brinton was a good fellow, devoted to scientific agriculture and the growing of small fruits; a man of a most practical mind. I knew him and his associates very well, and had no hesitation in calling upon them.

At the end of the month, as I had previously resolved, I brought my course of physical transfers to a close; and it was with no little anxiety that I arose one morning from my bed with my mind determined to bear in my own proper person all the ills of which I was possessed.

I walked across the room. It may appear strange, but I must admit that it was with a feeling of satisfaction that I felt a twinge. It was but a little twinge, but yet I felt it, and this was something that had not happened to me for a month.

"It was not fancy then," I said to myself, "that gave me this precious relief, this month of rare delight and profit; it was the operation of the outstretching power of the mind. I owe you much happiness, you little man with the big head whom I met in the Kursaal, and if you were here I would make you admit that I can truly believe in myself."

The next day I was better, with only an occasional touch of the old disorder; and in a few days I was free from it altogether, and could walk as well as ever I could in my life.

I returned to America strong and agile, and with a portfolio full of suggestive sketches. One of these was the back hair and part of the side face of a girl who was engaged in sketching in a mountainous region. But this I tore up on the voyage.

WEST.

I WILL now relate the events which took place in America, among the people in whom I was most interested, while I, a few thousand miles to the east, was enjoying my month of excursion and art work in the mountains of Switzerland.

On my return to my old associates I had intended to state to all of them, in turn, that I owed my delightful holiday to the fact that I had been able to transfer to them the physical disability which had prevented me from making use of the opportunities offered me by the Alps and the vales of Helvetia. But by conversation with one and another I gradually became acquainted with certain interesting facts which determined me to be very cautious in making disclosures regarding the outreaching power of my will.

No one of my friends was so much affected by my departure for Europe as that dear girl Kate Balthis, although I had no idea at the time that this was so. It was not that she was opposed to my going; on the contrary, it was she who had most encouraged me to persevere in my intention to visit Europe, and to conquer or disregard the many obstacles to the plan which rose up before me. She had taken a great interest in my artistic career, and much more personal interest in me than I had dared to suppose. She had imagined, and I feel that she had a perfect right to do so, that I felt an equal interest in her; and when I went away without a word more than any friend might say to another, the girl was hurt. It was not a deep wound; it was more in the nature of a rebuff. She felt a slight sense of humiliation, and wondered if she had infused more warmth into her intercourse with me than was warranted by the actual quality of our friendship. But she cherished no resentment, and merely put away an almost finished interior, in which I had painted a fair but very distant landscape seen through a partly opened window, and set herself to work on a fresh canvas.

Chester Parkman, the artist-athlete whom I have mentioned, was always fond of Kate's society; but after my departure he came a great deal more frequently to her studio than before; and he took it into his head that he would like to have his portrait painted by her. I had never supposed that Parkman's mind was capable of such serviceable subtlety as this, and I take the opportunity here to give him credit for it. Kate's forte was clearly portraiture, although she did not confine herself at that time to this class of work; and she was well pleased to have such an admirable subject as Chester Parkman, who, if he had not been an artist himself, might have made a very comfortable livelihood by acting as a model for other artists. This portrait-painting business, of which I should have totally disapproved had I known of it, brought them together for an hour every day; and, although Kate had two or three pupils, they worked in an adjoining room, separated by drapery from her own studio; and this gave Parkman every opportunity of making himself as agreeable as he could be. His method of accomplishing this, I have reason to believe, was by looking as well as he could rather than by conversational efforts. But he made Kate agreeable to him in a way of which at the time she knew nothing. He so arranged his position that a Venetian mirror in a corner gave him an admirable view of Kate's face as she sat at her easel. Thus, as she studied his features, his eyes dwelt more and more fondly upon hers, though she noticed it not. This sort of thing went on till Parkman found himself in a very bad way. The image of Kate rose up before him when he was not in her studio, and it had such an influence upon him that, if I may so put it, he gradually sunk his lungs, and let his heart rise to the surface. He imagined, though with what reason I am not prepared to say, that he could perceive in Kate's countenance indications of much admiration of her subject, and he flattered himself this was not confined to her consideration of him as a model. In fact, he found that he was very much in love with the girl. If he had been a wise man, he would have postponed proposing to her until his portrait was finished, for if she refused him he would lose both picture and painter. But he was not a wise man, and one day he made up his mind that as soon as she had finished the corner of his mouth, at which she was then at work, he would abandon his pose, and tell her how things stood with him. But a visitor came in, and prevented this plan from being carried out. This interruption, however, was merely a postponement. Parkman determined that on the next day he would settle the matter with Kate the moment he arrived at the studio, or as soon, at least, as he was alone with her.

If he had known the state of Kate's mind at this time, he would have been very much encouraged. I do not mean to say that any tenderness of sentiment towards him was growing up within her, but she had begun to admire very much this fine, handsome fellow. She took more pleasure in working at his portrait than in any other she had yet done. A man, she had come to think, to be true to art and to his manhood, should look like this one.

Thus it was that although Kate Balthis had not yet thought of her model with feelings that had become fond, it could not be denied that her affections, having lately been obliged to admit that they had no right to consider themselves occupied, were not in a condition to repel a new comer. And Parkman was a man who, when he had made up his mind to offer his valued self, would do it with a vigor and earnestness that could not easily be withstood.

It was a long time before Chester Parkman went to sleep that night, so engaged was he in thinking upon what he was going to do on the morrow. But, shortly after he arose the next morning, he was attacked by a very queer feeling in his left leg, which made it decidedly unpleasant for him when he attempted to walk. Indisposition of any kind was exceedingly unusual with the young athlete, but he knew that under the circumstances the first thing necessary for his accurately developed muscles was absolute rest, and this he gave them. He sent a note to Kate, telling her what had happened to him, and expressing his great regret at not being able to keep his appointment for the day. He would see her, however, at the very earliest possible moment that this most unanticipated disorder would allow him. He sent for a trainer, and had himself rubbed and lotioned, and then betook himself to a pipe, a novel, and a big easy-chair, having first quieted his much perturbed soul by assuring it that if he did not get over this thing in a few days, he would write to Kate, and tell her in the letter all he had intended to say.

The next day, much to his surprise, he arose perfectly well. He walked, he strode, he sprang into the air; there was absolutely nothing the matter with him. He rejoiced beyond his power of expression, and determined to visit Kate's studio even earlier than the usual hour; but before he was ready to start he received a note from her, which stated that she had been obliged to stay at home that day on account of a sudden attack of something like rheumatism, and therefore, even if he thought himself well enough, he need not make the exertion necessary to go all the way up to her studio. This note was very prettily expressed, and on the first reading of it Parkman could see nothing in it but a kind desire on the part of the writer that he should know there would be no occasion for him to do himself a possible injury by mounting to her lofty studio before he was entirely recovered. Of course she could not know, he thought, that he would be able to come that day, but it was very good of her to consider the possible contingency.

But, after sitting down and reflecting on the matter for ten or fifteen minutes, Parkman took a different view of the note. He now perceived that the girl was making fun of him. What imaginable reason was there for believing that she, a perfectly healthy person, should be suddenly afflicted by a rheumatism which apparently was as much like that of which he had told her the day before as one pain could be like another. Yes, she was making game of the muscles and sinews on which he prided himself. She did not believe the excuse he had given, and trumped up this ridiculous ailment to pay him back in his own coin. Chester Parkman was not easily angered, but he allowed this note to touch him on a tender point. It seemed to intimate that he would asperse his own physical organization in order to get an excuse for not keeping an appointment. To accuse him of such disloyalty was unpardonable. He was very indignant, and said to himself that he would give Miss Balthis some time to come to her senses; and that if she were that kind of a girl, it would be very well for him to reflect. He wrote a coldly expressed note to Kate, in which he said that, as far as he was concerned, he would not inconvenience her by giving her even the slightest reason for coming to her studio during the continuance of her most inexplicable malady.

Mr. Chester Parkman's mind might have been much more legitimately disturbed had he known that during the night before Kate had been lying awake, and had been thinking of me. She had heard that day from a friend, to whom I had written, of the great misfortune which had happened to me in Switzerland; and she had been thinking, dear girl, that if it were possible how gladly would she bear my trouble for a time, and give me a chance to enjoy that lovely land which I had tried so hard to reach. And if he had been told that at that very time, as I lay awake in the early morning, the idea had come into my head, although most instantly dismissed, that I should like to be beholden to Kate for a day of Alpine pleasure, he would reasonably have wondered what that had to do with it.

After I had become acquainted with these facts, I asked young Tom Latham, the oarsman, to whom I supposed I had transferred my physical condition on the day after I walked with Parkmanic legs to see the sun rise, if he had been at all troubled with rheumatism during the past few months. He replied with some asperity that he had been as right as a trivet straight along; and why in the world did I imagine he was subject to rheumatism!

Of course Kate was annoyed when she received Parkman's note. She saw that he had taken offence at something, although she had no idea what it was. But she did not allow this to trouble her long, and said to herself that if Mr. Parkman was angry with her she was very sorry, but she would be content to postpone work on the portrait until he should recover his good humor.

When she had retired that night she had determined

that, if she should not be well enough to go to her studio in a few days, she would send for some of her working materials and try to paint in her room. But the next morning she arose perfectly well.

If, however, she had known what was going to happen, she would have preferred spending another day in her pleasant chamber with her books and sewing. For, about eleven o'clock in the morning, there walked into her studio Professor Dynard, a gentleman who for some time had taken a great deal of interest in her and her work.

She had usually been very well pleased to talk to him, for he was a man of wide information and good judgment. But this morning there seemed to be something about him which was not altogether pleasant. In the first place, he stood before the unfinished portrait of Chester Parkman, regarding it with evident displeasure. For some minutes he said nothing, but hemmed and grunted. Presently he turned and remarked, "I don't like it."

"What is the matter with it?" asked Kate from the easel at which she was at work. "Have I not caught the likeness?"

"Oh, that is good enough as far as it goes," said the Professor. "Very good indeed! too good! You are going to make an admirable picture. But I wish you had another subject."

"Why, I thought myself extraordinarily fortunate in getting so good a one!" exclaimed Kate. "Is he not an admirable model?"

"Of course he is," said the professor, "but I don't

like to see you painting a young fellow like Parkman. Now, don't be angry," he continued, taking a seat near her and looking around to see if the curtain of the pupils' room was properly drawn. "I take a great interest in your welfare, Miss Balthis, and my primary object in coming here this morning is to tell you so; and, therefore, you must not be surprised that I was somewhat annoyed when I found that you were painting young Parkman's portrait. I don't like you to be painting the portraits of young men, Miss Balthis, and I will tell you why." And then he drew his chair a little nearer to her, and offered himself in marriage.

It must be rather awkward for a young lady artist to be proposed to at eleven o'clock in the morning, when she is sitting at her easel, one hand holding her palette and maul-stick, and the other her brush, and with three girl pupils on the other side of some moderately heavy drapery, probably listening with all their six ears. But in Kate's case the peculiarity of the situation was emphasized by the fact that this was the first time that any one had ever proposed to her. She had expected me to do something of the kind; and two days before, although she did not know it, she had just missed a declaration from Parkman; but now it was really happening, and a man was asking her to marry him. And this man was Professor Dynard! Had Kate been in the habit of regarding him with the thousand eyes of a fly, never, with a single one of those eyes, would she have looked upon him as a lover. But she turned towards him, and sat up very straight, and listened to all he had to say.

The Professor told a very fair story. He had long admired Miss Balthis, and had ended by loving her. He knew very well that he was no longer a young man, but he thought that if she would carefully consider the matter, she would agree with him that he was likely to make her a much better husband than the usual young man could be expected to make. In the first place, the object of his life, as far as fortune was concerned, had been accomplished, and he was ready to devote the rest of his days to her, her fortune, and her happiness. He would not ask her to give up her art, but, on the contrary, would afford her every facility for work and study under the most favorable circumstances. He would take her to Europe, to the isles of the sea, — wherever she might like to go. She could live in the artistic heart of the world, or in any land where she might be happy. He was a man both able and free to devote himself to her. He had money enough, and he was not bound by circumstances to special work or particular place. Through him the world would be open to her, and his greatest happiness should be to see her enjoy her opportunities. "More than that," he continued, "I want you to remember that, although I am no longer in my first youth, I am very strong, and enjoy excellent health. This is something you should consider very carefully in making an alliance for life; for it would be most unfortunate for you if you should marry a man who, early in life, should become incapacitated from pursuing his career, and you should find yourself obliged to provide, not only for yourself, but for him."

This, Kate knew very well, was intended as a reference to me. Professor Dynard had reason to believe I was much attached to Kate, and he had heard exaggerated accounts of my being laid up with rheumatism in Switzerland. It was very good in him to warn her against a man who might become a chronic invalid on her hands; but Kate said nothing to him, and let him go on.

"And even these devotees of muscularity," said the Professor, "these amateur athletes, are liable to be stricken down at any moment by some unforeseen disease. I do not wish to elevate the body above the mind, Miss Balthis, but these things should be carefully considered. You should marry a man who is not only in vigorous health, but is likely to continue so. And now, my dear Miss Balthis, I do not wish you to utter one word in answer to what I have been saying to you. I want you to consider, carefully and earnestly, the proposition I have made. Do not speak now, I beg of you, for I know I could not expect at this moment a favorable answer. I want you to give your calm judgment an opportunity to come to my aid. On the day after to-morrow I will come to receive your answer. Good-bye."

During that afternoon and the next day Kate thought of little but of the offer of marriage which had been made to her. Sometimes she regretted that she had not been bold enough to interrupt him with a refusal, and so end the matter. And then, again, she fell to thinking upon the subject of love, thinking and thinking. Naturally her first thoughts fell upon me. But

I had not spoken, nor had I written. This could not be accidental. It had a meaning which she ought not to allow herself to overlook. She found, too, while thus turning over the contents of her mind, that she had thought a little, a very little she assured herself, about Chester Parkman. She admitted that there was something insensibly attractive about him, and he had been extremely attentive and kind to her. But even if her thoughts had been inclined to dwell upon him, it would have been ridiculous to allow them to do so now, for in some way she had offended him, and might never see him again. He must be of a very irritable disposition.

And then there came up before her visions of Europe and of the isles of the sea; of a life amid the art wonders of the world, — a life with every wish gratified, every desire made possible. Professor Dynard had worked much better than she had supposed at the time he was working. He had not offered her the kind of love she had expected, should love ever be offered, but he had placed before her, immediately and without reserve, everything to which she had expected to attain by the labors of a life. All this was very dangerous thinking for Kate; the fortifications of her heart were being approached at a very vulnerable point. When she started independently in life, she did not set out with the determination to fall in love, or to have love made to her, or to be married, or anything of the kind. Her purpose was to live an art life; and to do that as she wished to do it, she would have to work very hard and wait very long. But now, all she had to do was to give a little nod, and the hope of the future would be the fact of the present. Even her own self would be exalted. "What a different woman should I be," she thought, "in Italy or in Egypt." This was a terribly perilous time for Kate. The temptation came directly into the line of her hopes and aspirations. It tinged her mind with a delicately spreading rosiness.

The next morning when she went to her studio she found there a note from Professor Dynard, stating that he could not keep his appointment with her that day on account of a sudden attack of something like rheumatism, which made it impossible to leave his room. This indisposition was not a matter of much importance, he wrote, and would probably disappear in a few days, when he would hasten to call upon her. He begged that in the mean time she would continue the consideration of the subject on which he had spoken to her; and hoped very earnestly that she would arrive at a conclusion which should be favorable to him, and which, in that case, he most sincerely believed would also be favorable to herself.

When she read this, Kate leaned back in her chair and laughed. "After all he said the other day about the danger of my getting a husband who would have to be taken care of, this is certainly very funny!" She forgot the rosy hues which had been insensibly tinting her dreams of the future on the day before, and only thought of a middle-aged gentleman, with a little bald place on the top of his head, who was subject to rheumatism, and probably very cross when he was obliged to stay in the house. "It is a shame," she said to herself, "to allow the poor old gentleman to worry his mind about me any longer. It will be no more than a deception to let him lie at home and imagine that as soon as he is well he can come up here and get a favorable answer from me. I'll write him a note immediately and settle the matter." And this she did, and thereby escaped the greatest danger to herself to which she had ever been exposed.

Nearly all Kate's art friends had been very much interested in her portrait of Chester Parkman, which, in its nearly completed state, was the best piece of work she had done. Among these friends was Bufford, whose pupil Kate had been, and to whom she had long looked up, not only as to a master, but as to a dear and kind friend. Mrs. Bufford, too, was extremely fond of Kate, and was ever ready to give her counsel and advice, but not in regard to art, which subject she resigned entirely to her husband. It was under Mrs. Bufford's guidance that Kate, when she first came to the city from her home in the interior of the State, selected her boarding-house, her studio, and her church. More than half of her Sundays were spent with these good friends, and they had always considered it their duty to watch over her as if her parents had appointed them her guardians. Bufford was greatly disappointed when he found that the work on Parkman's portrait had been abruptly broken off. He had wished Kate to finish it in time for an approaching exhibition, where he knew it would attract great attention, both from the fact that the subject was so well known in art circles and in society, and because it was going to be, he believed, a most admirable piece of work. Kate had explained to him, as far as she knew, how matters stood. Mr. Parkman had suddenly become offended with her, why she knew not. He was perfectly well and able to come, she said, for some of her friends had seen him going about as usual; but he did not come to her, and she certainly did not intend to ask him to do so. Bufford shook his head a good deal at this, and when he went home and told his wife about it, he expressed his opinion that Kate was not to blame in the matter.

"That young Parkman," he said, "is extremely touchy, and he has an entirely too good opinion of himself; and by indulging in some of his cranky notions he is seriously interfering with Kate's career, for she has nothing on hand except his portrait which I would care to have her exhibit."

"Now don't you be too sure," said Mrs. Bufford, "about Kate not being to blame. Young girls, without the slightest intention, sometimes do and say things which are very irritating, and Kate is just as high-spirited as Parkman is touchy. I have no doubt that the whole quarrel is about some ridiculous trifle, and could be smoothed over with a few words, if we could only get the few words said. I was delighted when I heard she was painting Chester's portrait, for I hoped the work would result in something much more desirable even than a good picture."

"I know you always wanted her to marry him," said Bufford.

"Yes, and I still want her to do so. And a little

piece of nonsense like this should not be allowed to break off the best match I have ever known."

"Since our own," suggested her husband.

"That is understood," she replied. "And now, do you know what I think is our duty in the premises? We should make it our business to heal this quarrel, and bring these young people together again. I am extremely anxious that no time should be lost in doing this, for it will not be long before young Clinton will be coming home. He was to stay away only three months altogether."

"And you are afraid he will interfere with your plans?" said Bufford.

"Indeed I am," answered his wife. "For a long time Kate and he have been very intimate, — entirely too much so, — and I was very glad when he went away, and gave poor Chester a chance. Of course there is nothing settled between them so far, because if there had been Clinton would never have allowed that portrait to be thought of."

"Jealous wretch!" remarked Bufford.

"You need not joke about it," said his wife. "It would be a most deplorable thing for Kate to marry Clinton. He has, so far, made no name for himself in art, and no one can say that he ever will. He is poor, and has nothing on earth but what he makes, and it is not probable that he will ever make anything. And, worse than all that, he has become a chronic invalid. I have heard about his condition in Switzerland."

"And having originally very little," said her husband, "and having lost the only valuable thing he possessed, you would take away from him even what he expected to have."

"He has no right to expect it," said Mrs. Bufford, "and it would be a wicked and cruel thing for him to endeavor to take Kate away from a man like Chester Parkman. Chester is rich, he is handsome, he is in perfect health, and to a girl with an artistic mind like Kate he should be a constant joy to look upon."

"But," said Bufford, "why don't you leave Kate to find out these superiorities for herself?"

"It would never do at all. Don't you see how she has let the right man go on account of some trifling misunderstanding? And Clinton will come home, and find that he has the field all to himself. Now I'll tell you what I want you to do. You must go to Kate to-morrow, find out what this trouble is about, and represent to her that she ought not to allow a little misunderstanding to interfere with her career in art."

"Why don't you go yourself?" said Bufford.

"That is out of the question. I could not put the matter on an art basis, and anything else would rouse Kate's suspicions. And, besides, I want you afterwards to go to Parkman, and talk to him; and, of course, I could not do that."

"Very well," said Bufford, "I am going to see them both to-morrow, and will endeavor to make things straight between them; but I don't wish to be considered as having anything to do with the matrimonial part of the affair. What I want is to have Kate finish that picture in time for the exhibition."

"You attend to that," said his wife, "and the matrimonial part will take care of itself."

But Bufford did not see either Kate or Parkman the next day, being prevented from leaving his room by a sudden attack of something like rheumatism. He was a man of strong good sense and persuasive speech, and I think he would have had no difficulty in bringing Parkman and Kate together again; and if this had happened, I am very certain that Parkman would have lost no time in declaring his passion. What would have resulted from this, of course, I cannot say; but it must be remembered that Kate at that time supposed that she had made a great mistake in regard to my sentiments towards her. In fact, if Bufford had seen the two young people that day, I am afraid, I am very much afraid that everything would have gone wrong.

The next day Bufford did see Kate, and easily obtained her permission to call on Parkman, and endeavor to find out what it was that had given him umbrage; but as the young athlete had started that very morning for a trip to the West, Bufford was obliged to admit to himself, very reluctantly, that it was probably useless to consider any further the question of Kate's finishing his portrait in time for the exhibition.

When I returned to America, and at the very earliest possible moment presented myself before Kate, I had not been ten seconds in her company before I perceived that I was an accepted lover. How I perceived this I will not say, for every one who has been accepted can imagine it for himself; but I will say that, although raised to the wildest pitch of joy by the discovery, I was very much surprised at it. I had never told the girl I loved her. I had never asked her to love me. But here it was, all settled, and Kate was my own dear love. Of course, feeling as I did towards her, it was easy for me to avoid any backwardness of demeanor, which might indicate to her that I was surprised, and I know that not for a moment did she suspect it. Before the end of our interview, however, I found out how I had been accepted without knowing it. It had been on account of the letter I had written Kate from Switzerland. In this very carefully constructed epistle I had hinted at a great many things which I had been careful not to explain, not wishing to put upon paper the story of my series of wonderful deliverances, which I intended with my own mouth to tell to Kate. It was a subtly quiet letter, with a substratum of hilariousness, of enthusiasm, surging beneath it, which sometimes showed through the thin places in the surface. Of course, writing to Kate, my mind was full of her, as well as of my deliverances, and in my hypersubtlety I so expressed my feelings in regard to the latter of these subjects that it might easily have been supposed to pertain to the first. In fact, when I afterwards read this letter I did not wonder at all that the dear girl thought it was a declaration of love. That she made the mistake I shall never cease to rejoice; for, after leaving Switzerland, I should not have been able, involuntarily and unconsciously, to ward off until my return the attacks of possible lovers.

From day to day I met nearly all the persons who, without having the slightest idea that they were doing anything of the kind, had been of such wonderful service to me while I was abroad; and I never failed to make particular inquiries in regard to their health the past summer. Most of them replied that they had been very well as a general thing, although now and then they might have been under the weather for a day or two. Few of my friends were people who were given to remembering ailments past and gone, and if I had needed any specific information from them in regard to any particular day on which they had been confined to the house by this or that slight disorder, I should not have obtained it.

But when I called upon Henry Brinton, the editor of "Our Mother Earth," I received some very definite and interesting information.

"Everything has gone on pretty much as usual since you left," he said, "except that about a month ago we had a visitation of a curious sort of epidemic rheumatism, which actually ran through the office. It attacked me first, but as I understand such things and know very well that outward applications are of no possible use, I took the proper medicine, and in one day, sir, I was entirely cured. The next day, however, Barclay, our book-keeper, was down with it, or, rather, he was obliged to stay at home on account of it. I immediately sent him my bottle of medicine, and the next day he came down to the office perfectly well. After him Brown, Simmons, Cummings, and White, one after another, were all attacked in the same way, but each was cured by my medicine in a day. The malady, however, seemed gradually to lose its force, and Cummings and White were only slightly inconvenienced, and were able to come to the office."

All this was very plain to me. Brinton's medicine was indeed the proper remedy for my ailment, and had gradually cured it, so that when I resumed it after my month's exemption, there was very little left of it, and this soon died out of itself. If I could only have known this, I would have sent it over to Brinton in the first instance.

In the course of time I related to Kate the strange series of incidents which had finally brought us together. I am sorry to say she did not place entire belief in the outreaching powers of my mind. She thought that the relief from my disability was due very much to imagination.

"How," I said, "do you account for those remarkable involuntary holidays of Parkman, yourself, and the others, which were so opportune for me?"

"Things did happen very well for you," she said, "although I suppose a great many other people have had a series of lucky events come into their lives. But even if this were all true, I do not think it turned out exactly as it should have done in a moral point of view. Of course I am delighted, you poor boy, that you should have had that charming month in Switzerland, after all the trouble you had gone through; but wasn't it a little selfish to pass off your disability upon your friends without asking them anything about it?"

"Well," said I, "it may be that if this affair were

viewed from a purely moral stand-point, there was a certain degree of selfishness about it, and it ought to have turned out all wrong for me. But we live in a real world, my dear, and it turned out all right."

"*Mr. Stockton has written a book which you can't discuss without laughing; and that is proof enough of its quality.*"
—N. Y. TRIBUNE.

THE LATE MRS. NULL.

By FRANK R. STOCKTON.

One Volume. 12mo. Cloth. $1.50.

"THE LATE MRS. NULL" is one of those fortunate books that goes beyond all expectation. Even those readers whose hopes have been raised the highest have before them—especially in the fact that they receive the story complete and at once, without intermediate serial publication—such an enjoyment as they hardly foresee.

It is enough to say of the scene that it is chiefly in Virginia, to show the possibilities of local character-drawing open to Mr. Stockton in addition to his other types; and to say that every character is full of the most ingenious and delicious originality is altogether needless. In an increasing scale, the situations are still more complicated, ingenious, and enjoyable than the characters; and finally, the plot is absolutely baffling in its clever intricacy yet apparent simplicity—a true device of Mr. Stockton's tireless fancy.

"We congratulate the novel reader upon the feast there is in 'The Late Mrs. Null.'"—*Hartford Post*.

"We can assure prospective readers that their only regret after finishing the book will be that never again can they hope for the pleasure of reading it again for the first time."—*The Critic*.

"Original, bright, and full of the author's delicate humor."—*New York Journal of Commerce*.

"'The Late Mrs. Null' is delicious."—*Boston Journal*.

CHARLES SCRIBNER'S SONS,

743 & 745 Broadway, New-York.

Mrs. Burnett's Novels.

UNIFORM LIBRARY EDITION

Six vols., extra cloth. Price, per set, $7.50

SOLD SEPARATELY

THAT LASS O' LOWRIE'S.

One volume, 12mo, extra cloth, - - $1.25

"We know of no more powerful work from a woman's hand in the English language, not even excepting the best of George Eliot's."—*Boston Transcript.*

A FAIR BARBARIAN.

One volume, 12mo, extra cloth, - - $1.25

"A particularly sparkling story, the subject being the young heiress of a Pacific silver-mine, thrown amid the very proper petty aristocracy of an English rural town."—*Springfield Republican.*

THROUGH ONE ADMINISTRATION.

One volume, 12mo, extra cloth, - - $1.50

"The pathetic fervor which Mrs. Burnett showed so fully in 'That Lass o' Lowrie's' is exhibited in many a touching scene in her new story, which is only to be found fault with because it is too touching."—*London Athenæum.*

LOUISIANA.

One volume, 12mo, extra cloth, - - $1.25

"We commend this book as the product of a skillful, talented, well-trained pen. Mrs. Burnett's admirers are already numbered by the thousand, and every new work like this one can only add to their number."—*Chicago Tribune.*

HAWORTH'S

One volume, 12mo, extra cloth, - - $1.25

"It is but faint praise to speak of 'Haworth's' as merely a good novel. It is one of the few great novels."—*Hartford Courant.*

SURLY TIM,
AND OTHER STORIES.

One volume, 12mo, extra cloth, - - $1.25

"Each of these narratives have a distinct spirit, and can be profitably read by all classes of people. They are told not only with true art but with deep pathos."—*Boston Post.*

A BEAUTIFUL NEW EDITION.

By FRANK R. STOCKTON.
ILLUSTRATED BY A. B. FROST.

One vol., 12mo, - $2.00.

The new Rudder Grange has not been illustrated in a conventional way. Mr. Frost has given us a series of interpretations of Mr. Stockton's fancies, which will delight every appreciative reader,—sketches scattered through the text; larger pictures of

the many great and memorable events, and everywhere quaint ornaments. It is, on the whole, one of the best existing specimens of the complete supplementing of one another by author and artist. The book is luxurious in the best sense of the word, admirable in typography, convenient in size, and bound in a capital cover of Mr. Frost's design.

For sale by all booksellers, or sent, post-paid, by the publishers,

CHARLES SCRIBNER'S SONS,
743 & 745 Broadway, New-York.

*"Stockton has the knack, perhaps genius would be a better word, of writing in the easiest of colloquial English without descending to the plane of the vulgar or commonplace. * * * With the added charm of a most delicate humor, his stories become irresistibly attractive."—* PHILADELPHIA TIMES.

STOCKTON'S STORIES

THE LADY, OR THE TIGER?
AND OTHER STORIES

One volume, 12mo, cloth, . . . $1.25

THE LADY, OR THE TIGER?
THE TRANSFERRED GHOST
THE SPECTRAL MORTGAGE
OUR ARCHERY CLUB
THAT SAME OLD 'COON
OUR STORY   HIS WIFE'S DECEASED SISTER
MR. TOLMAN
ON THE TRAINING OF PARENTS
OUR FIRE-SCREEN
A PIECE OF RED CALICO
EVERY MAN HIS OWN LETTER-WRITER

THE CHRISTMAS WRECK
AND OTHER STORIES

One volume, 12mo, cloth, . . . $1.25

THE CHRISTMAS WRECK
A STORY OF ASSISTED FATE (*in two parts*)
AN UNHISTORIC PAGE
A TALE OF NEGATIVE GRAVITY
THE REMARKABLE WRECK OF THE "THOMAS HYKE"
MY BULL-CALF
THE DISCOURAGER OF HESITANCY
A BORROWED MONTH (*East and West*)
THE CLOVERFIELD'S CARRIAGE

For sale by all booksellers, or sent post-paid, by the publishers,

CHARLES SCRIBNER'S SONS
743 and 745 Broadway, New York

www.ingramcontent.com/pod-product-compliance
Lightning Source LLC
Chambersburg PA
CBHW031353230426
43670CB00006B/532